Beyond Love and Loyalty

Elizabeth Nowell

Beyond Love and Loyalty

The Letters of Thomas Wolfe

and Elizabeth Nowell

Together with "No More Rivers"

A Story by Thomas Wolfe

Edited by Richard S. Kennedy

The University of North Carolina Press

Chapel Hill and London

Manufactured in the United States of America

Letters of Thomas Wolfe © 1983 Paul Gitlin,
Administrator, C.T.A.,
Estate of Thomas Wolfe

Letters of Elizabeth Nowell © 1983
Clara Perkins Stites

Library of Congress Cataloging in Publication Data

Wolfe, Thomas, 1900–1938.
  Beyond love and loyalty.

  Includes index.
    1. Wolfe, Thomas, 1900–1938—Correspondence.
2. Nowell, Elizabeth—Correspondence. 3. Novelists,
American—20th century—Correspondence. 4. Literary
agents—United States—Correspondence. I. Nowell,
Elizabeth. II. Wolfe, Thomas, 1900–1938. No more
rivers. 1983. III. Kennedy, Richard S. IV. Title.
PS3545.O337Z49 1983   813'.52 [B]   82-15939
ISBN 0-8078-1545-4

For
My Own Liddy

Contents

Acknowledgments

Grateful acknowledgment is here made

To Paul Gitlin, Administrator C. T. A. of the Estate of Thomas Wolfe, for permission to publish the letters of Thomas Wolfe and his story, "No More Rivers."

To Clara Perkins Stites for permission to publish the letters of her mother, Elizabeth Nowell Perkins.

To W. H. Bond, librarian of Houghton Library, Harvard University, for permissions and for making available the Wolfe and Nowell materials in the William B. Wisdom Collection; and to Rodney Dennis, Marte Shaw, Suzanne Currier, Thomas Noonan, and the staff of the Reading Room for their help.

To H. G. Jones, librarian of the North Carolina Collection, University of North Carolina Library, Chapel Hill, for permissions and for making available the letters of Wolfe and Nowell in the collection.

To Charles Scribner's Sons and to William Heinemann Ltd. for permission to reprint those letters or portions of letters that appeared in the *The Letters of Thomas Wolfe*, collected and edited by Elizabeth Nowell. Copyright © 1956 Edward C. Aswell, Administrator C. T. A. of the Estate of Thomas Wolfe.

To Nancy Hale, the late Clara Howland Nowell, and the Bryn Mawr Alumni Association for information about Elizabeth Nowell.

To Andrea Brown, librarian of St. Mary's College Library, Raleigh, North Carolina, whose invitation to me to talk on Thomas Wolfe at the St. Mary's Wolfe Fest in 1979 led to the creation of this book.

To Robert Alan Watts and Nadia Kravchenko for skillful typewriting services.

Introduction: A Unique Relationship
by Richard S. Kennedy

One day in 1949 when I was a graduate student at Harvard, I received a letter from Elizabeth Nowell announcing that she was under contract to prepare an edition of Thomas Wolfe's letters for Scribner's and asking me if she could read the seminar paper I had written about Wolfe's Harvard years. In this way we began a ten-year friendship and practice of mutual aid as I went ahead with my Ph.D. dissertation and later writings on Wolfe and she made visits to the Houghton Library working on the letters. Mutual aid, I said; "the blind leading the not-quite-so-blind,"[1] she called it. At that time, she was a middle-aged, somewhat stout woman with a twinkling eye and a bubbling laugh, ready to ruffle all the feathers of the library staff in the Houghton Library Reading Room. Her wit, high spirits, and irreverent language were immediately evident to anyone who met her, but one soon became aware of a warmth and delicate courtesy that were partly obscured by her effervescence.

As time went on, the generosity that she displayed toward me was unbelievable. Whenever she acquired a new Wolfe letter that reflected on his literary work in any way, she immediately made a typewritten copy and sent it to me; whenever I sent a query or two about an episode in Wolfe's life, I got back a two-or-three-page letter of single-spaced, accurate, and hilariously phrased information. We were soon on very easy terms. Her letters of inquiry to me always began in the breezy manner she had adopted toward me: "Hey, Toots, do you know if 'The Man on the Wheel' was part of 'K 19' or not?" or "Help I'm drowning in seas of only-guessed-at dates and wubber cement," and then she would go ahead and ask the question.[2] She told me to call her by her nickname, which was Liddy.

Her basic personality and her way of giving herself unstintingly to people whom she liked were somewhat hidden because of a role she had developed for herself during her years in the world of publishing. Since it was a man's world, she shouldered her way through it in the guise of a tough-minded, rough-tongued person who was not going to be pushed around. Her friend, Nancy Hale, remarked to me that Liddy Nowell was a solidly based, New England lady but that she cursed and swore more than any woman Nancy Hale had ever known. In any case, her letters to me were always liberally sprinkled with profanity. When I sent her a memoir about Wolfe written by one of his former classmates whose handwriting was very difficult to decipher, her letter in reply to me began, "Holy Jumping Jesus Christ, what writing!" and went on for a page that contained a lot of colorful phrasing. Her postscript explained: "This letter seems to me profaner than usual, but I've been writing formal letters to all the people I have photostats of letters to, so I just let myself relax I spose."[3]

That was Liddy Nowell in her late forties. Elizabeth Howland Nowell had been born June 10, 1904, near New Bedford, Massachusetts, of old New England stock on both sides. I always imagined that at least one of her ancestors had been the captain of a whaling vessel. She attended the Friends Academy there and later the Ethel Walker School, from which she was graduated in 1922. Her record was so outstanding that she was awarded the New England Scholarship, which she used to attend Bryn Mawr College, where she not only learned something about literature and writing but also acquired a feminist confidence that helped her to go her own way in the world. Her classmates remember her as an extremely lively and witty black-haired girl who loved dogs almost as much as she loved her friends.

She had always had a talent for writing, even winning a city-wide essay contest for high school students in New Bedford when she was only fifteen years old. After graduation from Bryn Mawr in 1926, she enrolled in a writing course at Columbia, trying her hand at fiction and writing book reviews for the *New Bedford Standard Times*. She later had some success publishing stories in *Harper's Bazaar* and *Redbook* under the pen name of "Sarah Grinnell." These literary leanings eventually landed her a job with *Scribner's Magazine* in 1928 where she became a reader of manuscripts. While on the *Scribner's* staff, she came to know the editors of the publishing house, Charles Scribner's Sons, which was in the same building on Fifth Avenue, and during the five years she worked there she developed an intimate knowledge of the business of both periodical and book publication.[4]

With this experience behind her, she joined the literary agency of Maxim Lieber in 1933, where she worked with such writers as Alvah Bessie, Daniel Fuchs, David de Jong, and Nancy Hale. It was at the Lieber agency that she first began to work with Thomas Wolfe in late 1933.

Wolfe had been struggling with *Of Time and the River* for four years then and had run through all the money that he had earned from *Look Homeward, Angel* and from occasional pieces published in *Scribner's Magazine* as well as a generous royalty advance on the as yet unfinished novel. Maxwell Perkins, always the paternal worrier about his Scribner authors, thought Wolfe ought to have an agent to help him place excerpts from his novel in various magazines as short fiction and thus provide him with some income. He remembered the bright, sassy Miss Nowell from her days at Scribner's and recommended that Wolfe go to the Lieber agency.

When Wolfe first talked at lunch with Maxim Lieber and Liddy Nowell, he was full of complaint about Scribner's. He had not forgotten that three years earlier the editors of the magazine had turned down the publication of his story, "In the Park," his first attempt to tell a story from the point of view of a woman. (The woman became known in his later novels as Esther Jack.) Maxim Lieber, who was a communist or a communist sympathizer, began then to fill Wolfe with talk about how badly The House of Scribner had been exploiting him. After all, he was one of their loyal workers and deserved to profit from the fruits of his agonized labors.

The first item Wolfe gave to Lieber for magazine sale was called "Boom Town," a first-person narrative in which a character named John Hawke described his return to his native city in the South. It had a great deal of material about the train ride, about alienation and return, about the way the real estate boom had changed the city, and about the members of his family, including a stuttering brother named Lee. In length, it was a short novel.

This was always Wolfe's trouble with periodical publication. His idea of a short fictional unit was 12,000 to 20,000 words, whereas magazine editors normally wanted to print short fiction of 7,000 words or less. Nowell and Lieber worked over "Boom Town" with Wolfe on three or more occasions, and, by the time he had revised and rewritten, it was a very different piece of work. Miss Nowell sold it to the *American Mercury*. Wolfe received $192 for it and remembered that *Scribner's Magazine* used to pay him $400 for a story of that length. He began to think twice about Lieber's talk of exploitation. But he also began to have a respect for Miss Nowell's opinions about the structure of short fiction when "Boom Town" was chosen to appear in the *O. Henry Memorial Prize Stories of 1934*.

Elizabeth Nowell next cast her critical eye on the story, "In the Park." Her memorandum about it is one of her earliest notes to Wolfe, and it reveals that she was tackling other problems besides length: since Wolfe's short pieces were always elements of his ever-lengthening autobiographical novels, they had to be altered in certain ways before they could stand by themselves. Her letter is filled with practical advice for adding details, for cutting out digressions, for developing a unifying motif about automobiles, and for tidying up the conclusion—all to make the piece more of a "story."[5] (I should add that before publication Wolfe took only two of her many suggestions: he deleted two short digressions.)

While at the Lieber agency, Miss Nowell was not able to do much for Wolfe. She placed a big chunk of *Of Time and the River* with *Redbook* for $750, but it had to be withdrawn because the book was scheduled for publication before the excerpt could appear in the magazine.

Miss Nowell's mother told me long ago that Whittaker Chambers had warned Elizabeth to get away from Lieber because of his Communist party associations. I do not think that is what motivated her to leave Lieber and set up her own agency, for she told me herself that she never paid much attention to Lieber's political views. But she did set out on her own in late 1934, taking Wolfe and others with her while the novelists of social protest like Alvah Bessie and Daniel Fuchs remained with Lieber. Early in 1935, after *Of Time and the River* had been sent to the printers, she read through Wolfe's treasury of manuscripts, picking out any items that she thought could stand by themselves as stories, and by mid-1935 about half of the items that now make up *From Death to Morning* had been sold to periodicals.

Since Wolfe's proposed stories usually had to be cut and altered in some way, it was a touchy proposition to work with him, and it is a tribute to Miss Nowell's tact that they could continue their association, working as they did. As we now know, Wolfe had a paranoid tendency that caused him to quarrel with almost all of his friends and well-wishers, sometimes even over trivial matters. For example, on one occasion he wondered aloud to Miss Nowell what the critics would say about *Of Time and the River*. "And I said," she later recalled, "that some of the left-wing critics might jump on him, but that if they did he should pay no attention to them, just go right on the way he was. He was a little drunk, not much, but evidently just enough to get suspicious and mixed up and get things wrong. Because ever after that, for years, whenever he was REALLY drunk, he'd call me up around 2 A.M. and say in a ghostly green-hornet kind of voice, 'You—said—my—book—would—fail!' and I would shout at him that what I actually said was so-and-so, and that anyway he was drunk and should go to bed."[6]

During these early years of their association, Miss Nowell would go across the Brooklyn Bridge to Wolfe's apartment on Columbia Heights at night, bringing with her a tin of Lucky Strikes—flat fifties, they were called in those days—which she and Wolfe would finish off while they worked. She also brought along her suggestions for cuts and changes in a story she thought had possibilities. Some he would accept; others not, and as they worked, she sat at the typewriter while he dictated revisions—or passages to be added. The next day she would have a secretary make a clean copy ready to be sent to a magazine. Wolfe accepted this guidance from her because he had learned that the editors would not take his work in its first form, and he knew that when he put the material back into his novels he could restore any of the cuts he had been forced to make.

One of Miss Nowell's most important contributions to Wolfe's career was her help in getting *The Story of a Novel* into existence as a published work. Wolfe had written a long preface to *Of Time and the River* about the experience of writing the book and working with Perkins in its final shaping, but Scribner's scrapped the preface. Later he used a lengthened version of this discarded preface for a lecture at the Colorado Writers' Conference in 1935. Miss Nowell took this manuscript of seventy-four pages, cut it down to half its size by slicing out whole paragraphs and reducing trios of adjectives or phrases to one, and sold it to the *Saturday Review of Literature*, where it appeared in three installments.

When Scribner's decided to publish the piece in book form, Wolfe went back to it and replaced many of the paragraphs Miss Nowell had cut, but he did not bother restoring all the missing adjectives and phrases. He also added a long section about the anxiety dreams that he had during the composition of the book. Thus the style of *The Story of a Novel* in its final form is predominantly an effective conversational presentation that rises to a stylistically heightened climax about the "Dreams of Guilt and Time" and on to an intense peroration about the place of the artist in America. Not only did Miss Nowell's assistance contribute to the artistic success of the book but without her enterprise it would never have got into print.

As it turned out, her work on *The Story of a Novel* caused the only ugly episode in their relationship. Since she had cajoled Wolfe into letting her work on the essay when nobody at Scribner's had the remotest notion of its ever being a book and since she had labored so long and hard on it, she felt that she was entitled to an agent's commission not just on the magazine sale but on book sales too, and she deferentially and tentatively asked Wolfe about it. He was apparently in one of his paranoid states when her letter came, and in his twisted way of looking at her request, he saw her as one more of the leeches of the world trying to drain him of his hard-earned royalties. He made one of his angry, half-drunken, midnight telephone calls and denounced her.

It was unjust and insulting, but Liddy Nowell suffered the attack and then stood up for her rights. More than any other letter in this book, her reply to Wolfe reveals her character—her devotion to the interests of the people she worked with, her dignity in the face of injustice, yet her willingness to bend in order to be utterly fair:

> I guess you really didn't mean what you said on the phone but it's two thirty and I can't go to sleep again until I get it off my chest, so here goes and I hope you don't mind. Because I can't help being terribly hurt if you really think I'm a leech sucking unearned commissions out of you, and I can't help objecting because I honestly don't think you realize how much time and effort it takes to do a job like "The Story of a Novel." Sure, you did speak to [Henry Seidel] Canby [the editor of the *Saturday Review*] about it yourself, but before that I'd done a helluva lot of work and so please let me retrace the whole history of it in self-justification.
>
> Way back in March 1935 when I was helping you get out of Brooklyn and was sorting the manuscript, you gave me part of the preface and said that there might be something in it and would I get the "artist in America" part back from Sanderson Vanderbilt. So after a letter and several phone calls I got it from him and kept it until you came back from Germany when I gave it to you, and you and Mr. Perkins left it in a bar somewhere. So then when you were going to Colorado you gave me the first half of the second, dictated version and said for me to see what I could do. Well, I knew the chances were only about four for a thing like that but anyway I thought it was so terribly fine that I took it to the hospital with me and cut it from about 15000 [words] to 7000. . . .
>
> I know you think cutting like that is easy, but it really is the hardest thing in the world and the one which takes most patience, going over and over and taking out just a few words at a time and putting back half of them in an effort to be sure not to slaughter your meaning, and then counting up the whole estimate and finding it STILL much too long and reading the whole thing over in a search for more words to come out and then estimating etc. etc. and with it always too long until at the end

of a good week's work you're sure that it's as tight as it can be without butchering. Oh Jesus, I'm not complaining because it's worth it in your case, but what I'm trying to say is that I spent tremendous effort on it. . . .

So then I sent the article to the Yale Review, they declined it, and I sold it to the Atlantic. Whereupon you told me there'd been a mistake and the second half was missing and brought it around to me and I cut that in a rush job from around 15000 to 7000, couldn't sell it to the Atlantic too, recalled it at your request and sent it to Canby after those two or three evening sessions with you, or rather one with you and two or three more waiting for you with you unhappy about coming and getting here late and making me feel like a goddamned old-maid school-teacher and bawling like a baby when you started to open my beer with my kid glove. . . .

I'm not complaining because you know damn well that the thrill of working on your stuff is worth it in the long run, but it does hurt my feelings terribly to be told that I'm no damn good and a parasite on you . . . because I think I deserve a commission on the thing all the way through instead of $15 on the Saturday Review sale when that barely covers my expense of hiring Curtin to relieve me from my regular work to do that last rush job of cutting the second half. Besides I really and honestly think that the book would have remained one of those things you were going to do some day, or that Perkins didn't have time to work in, unless I'd salvaged it and cut it and sold it and it had got such swell critical recognition. But it isn't any of that that matters so much as feeling that somebody hates you when you've done your goddamndest working for them and when the whole thing seems so unjust and bitter.

Well, this is just plain hysterical now and I know you hate hysterical women more than anything on earth . . . but when I'm so terribly unhappy about a thing the only way is to pour it out and get it over instead of letting it eat me and make me act like a goddamned crybaby sometime if I ran into you at Scribner's. I don't care so much about the money even though I do think it's only fair and if you still think I'm a blood-sucker after reading this attempt at justification, all right, I won't take the money. . . .[7]

She got the commission. And an apology.

During the next year, Miss Nowell helped Wolfe sell to high-paying magazines such items as "The Bell Remembered," "I Have a Thing to Tell You," and "Mr. Malone." The peak of this activity was reached when she sold "The Child by Tiger" to the *Saturday Evening Post* for $1,200 and "The Lost Boy" to *Redbook* for $1,500 (the equivalent of about $12,000 in the money of the early 1980s). But besides the marketing, she made her contribution to many of these works by whittling away at Wolfe's verbosity or by badgering him into doing it himself.

The letters accumulate a mountain of evidence to support this. About "The Child by Tiger," she writes: "I've been cutting like mad ever since it came and have got it down to ten thousand and a half by dint of cutting *very* stringently. The chances are you'll object to some of the cuts but anyway look it over." About "The Lost Boy," she writes: "I guess this will keep you out of mischief all right Saturday afternoon. I've cut the hell out of it but finally got it down to within 100 words of the forty pages [the editor] said it would have to be. A lot of places will probably make your heart bleed because I wouldn't have thought of cutting them except in desperation."[8]

Her practice was to bracket the proposed excisions with pencil marks on the typescript, put in the margin the number of words each bracketed cut would eliminate, and then add up the marginal figures at the bottom of each page. Wolfe in making his decisions was thus faced with numerical evidence staring at him; as a consequence, he usually followed her advice, except when the meanings he wanted to develop were harmed.

As time went on, that kind of discipline made its impact upon his writing style. His work became less oratorical and more conversational; as a result, the items destined for magazine publication became shorter, and Miss Nowell did not need to do so much minor surgery on his pages as she had two years earlier.

But she had other burdens. Because Wolfe had been sued for libel by Marjorie Dorman, who objected to her treatment as "Mad Maude" in the short novel "No Door," Miss Nowell had to take care to alter any character portraits that bore too realistic a likeness to the original. The correspondence about the sketch "Mr. Malone" for the *New Yorker* is filled with remarks about changing the details of character so that he would not resemble the Irish critic, Ernest Boyd, too closely.

In the same way she was faced with a very delicate situation when Wolfe began to write about the staff at Scribner's. The first of these stories, "No More Rivers," which has never been published, reflected on the personal life of Wallace Meyer, one of Scribner's editors. Wolfe sent her to consult with Meyer himself about it and later with

Perkins, who became very apprehensive because he knew that he was the source of many anecdotes about the Scribner's people whom Wolfe might be planning to treat satirically in his fiction. For a period of two years, Miss Nowell had to go over "No More Rivers" so many times that she confessed finally to having become too close to the story to be objective about any editorial suggestions that she made.

By 1937 Wolfe and Nowell were very close friends and professional associates. Wolfe was aware of, and deeply grateful for, not just the means of earning money that she had opened up for him but especially for the help and loyalty she had given him. This closeness also meant that when he broke with Perkins and Scribner's he began to turn to Miss Nowell for personal advice and to depend on her to take care of a great many of his needs of all sorts. He used her office address to receive his personal as well as his business mail. He called upon her to check with the Fire Department about the details of the fire on Park Avenue that he used for the climax of "The Party at Jack's." He asked her to write to Mrs. Aline Bernstein for him when she made inquiries about his whereabouts. He used Miss Nowell as a buffer between himself and Scribner's when Perkins or others asked about him and wished to know if he was doing a satirical job on the world of publishing. She willingly undertook all these minor responsibilities and in addition supplied Wolfe increasingly with the continuous encouragement about his writing that Perkins had provided.

She also took it upon herself to defend Wolfe or his interests when necessary. One instance is the trouble that arose about the last piece of Wolfe's that she handled in his lifetime. This is her version of it: "When Prologue to America came out in Vogue [magazine], those hammy pseudo-Whitmanesque subtitles in it—'O Rocky Mountains, O Chicago,' etc.—were *not* in Tom's manuscript, but were inserted without our permission by that old pansy of a [Frank] Crowninshield. And when Tom saw them he hit the ceiling, and I did too. They broke up the flow of the Prologue to America, and they were just plain ludicrous, and in such terribly bad taste. I called up Miss [Allene] Talmey, feature editor or somesuch of Vogue . . . and bawled hell out of her, and said what right did they have to take a piece by a writer like Wolfe and write their own two-bit spurious Whitman titles into it. She said, 'Why, Mister Crowninshield did that. It is the Vogue custom to break up long prose pieces with sub-titles.' And I said that it might be OK for stuff about ladies clothes, but that they had done irreparable harm to Tom's reputation, because the general reader would assume Tom had written them. 'O Rocky Mountains, my arse,' I said and hung up."[9]

When Wolfe received a new contract from Harper and Brothers for his novel-in-progress, *The Web and the Rock*, he was careful to have removed from it any clauses in which Harper encroached upon Elizabeth Nowell's rights as his agent. As he told her, "no one is going to take one little red penny of the old gotten gains which have enabled you thus far to wallow in luxury at my expense—no sir, by gum, not if I can help it." He ended by saying, "I know I've been a pain in your neck for the last two or three weeks, but . . . I think a better day is dawning for us both. Anyway, 'that is no agent, that is my friend' is the way I really feel, and in one way or another I'll try to live up to it."[10]

When Wolfe finally put together his huge assembly of manuscript that he called *The Web and the Rock*, planning to let his new editor at Harper, Edward Aswell, look it over, he passed the material on for Miss Nowell's perusal first, for it was still an unfinished draft. She had seen many parts of it before but had not seen enough to get any sense of the whole. Her response, in one of the last letters she wrote him before his death, is quite characteristic, and it also shows her genuine feeling about Wolfe's ability to give mythic expression to the spirit of America:

> It looks as if this was going to be fanmail. But ever since I was there Monday night I've been thinking how swell the first big hunk—and all the other later hunks—of the book are. I too am "honored to have read it," and, too, in the real sense of the words.
>
> So many reviewers have yapped so much about the "great American novel" and in connection with so many piddling writers that it sounds almost silly to use that phrase now. But again going back to the "real sense of the words," I think you're it, Toots. Because nobody else in the world could get the real flavor of those tough, salty, swell old guys like Bear and Zach and the way they talked and thought and lived so perfectly, with all the juice still there as if this was still the early rough and ready frontier America. And what's more, nobody in the world but you could bring that to life and then keep all your juice and understanding right in stride and perfect tune with the whole of changing history and come through to the swell and right-in-the-present-and-future stuff like the last parts of the book: the whole New York modern life, the literary racket, the German Nazi stuff, the ruined town and the Parson and police and— well, the whole analysis of the world right this minute.
>
> God knows if this sounds too grandiloquent because I've got

some sweeping phrases in what I've just ripped off above without premeditation. But honestly, they really fit here and they aren't grandiloquent because it's the truth, so help me God. . . .[11]

When Wolfe, happily savoring a vacation trip in the West, received Elizabeth Nowell's letter, it made him feel even more confident about the future. "I know a lot of swell people," he replied, "and I think you are one of them, and I am proud to know you are my friend."[12]

It was an unusual professional friendship, and perhaps one of the reasons it worked so well was that Miss Nowell had the good sense not to have any sexual relations with Wolfe and thus add the complications of such intimacy to her literary association with an emotionally unstable genius. Not that Wolfe did not make his try. "Tom was always horny as hell," she scribbled in the margin of one of my pages, "and you had to keep him at arm's length." Her keeping that distance made their working relationship a success. He always began his letters, "Dear Miss Nowell," and she began hers, "Dear Mr. Wolfe" or, later, "Dear Wolfe."

Because she had to be so ultra-careful of his feelings and because she had to put in so much more time and labor on his material than on that of any of her other authors, the question arises, Why did she continue to work with him and for him in this way? One hardheaded answer is that he was good for the commercial success of her agency. She attracted other clients because she was known as Thomas Wolfe's agent. But there is another answer related to this one: she was acting out of gratitude to him because Wolfe had stuck with her when she was first starting out on her own and not earning much income for either him or herself. But other more personal feelings were involved too. Anyone who reads their correspondence can see that she had an affection for him as if he were an occasionally exasperating but nevertheless loved younger brother. Finally, we must recognize that she always had a keen appreciation for his creative genius: it would be a valuable experience in anyone's life to be associated with, indeed participate in, creative activity of a major sort. This, after all, is what had drawn Perkins so close to Wolfe. That is, I think, the major reason why she continued to be Wolfe's editorial factotum.

Elizabeth Nowell continued her loyalty and service to Wolfe even after his death. She oversaw the publication of "The Western Journal" and "The Party at Jack's." She kept on trying to sell "No More Rivers" for magazine publication, although she was no longer at liberty to make any changes in it. Most important of all, she helped

Edward Aswell to understand the quirks, gaps, and discrepancies in the manuscript that Wolfe had left behind him and that Aswell in his initial bewilderment referred to as "a mess."

After 1939, there was a hiatus in Liddy Nowell's service to Wolfe's reputation, but she returned to him, in a sense, after her divorce from Charles Perkins, whom she had married during the war. After 1948, she lived at home in South Dartmouth, Massachusetts, with her two children and her mother but was persuaded to reenter the literary world once more as agent for Nancy Hale and, more important, to be the editor of Thomas Wolfe's letters. After six years' work on that project, she discovered she knew so much about Wolfe that she went ahead to write his biography, a task that she plugged away at for five years, going through a grave illness, surgery, weakness, and pain as she drew near the close. She completed her last chapters in 1959 at the time she was in the grip of terminal cancer, although she remained cheerful right to the end.[13] When Nancy Hale visited her in Massachusetts General Hospital shortly before her death, Liddy Nowell did not want to be part of a lugubrious scene. She had a chilled bottle of champagne waiting to greet her guest.

That was characteristic of the woman I knew in her last decade—tough, life-loving, always ready to do something for a friend. When my wife and I had our first child, we named her Elizabeth after my wife's favorite aunt. But we always called that little girl Liddy.

NOTES

1. Letter to R. S. Kennedy, August 7, 1950.
2. Letters to R. S. Kennedy, September 18, 1951, and January 5, 1951.
3. Letter to R. S. Kennedy, October 31, 1949.
4. Information about Elizabeth Nowell's early life is drawn from the *New Bedford Standard-Times*, February 26, 1920, and August 25, 1959; from the Bryn Mawr Alumnae Office; from interviews with Mrs. Clara Howland Nowell, Nancy Hale, and Elizabeth Nowell herself.
5. December 15, 1933, Houghton Library.
6. Letter to R. S. Kennedy, October 31, 1949.
7. April 21, 1936, Houghton Library.
8. March 4, 1937, and March 5, 1937, Houghton Library.
9. Letter to R. S. Kennedy, October 10, 1954.
10. December 29, 1937, Houghton Library.
11. May 11, 1938, Houghton Library.
12. June 19 [1938], Houghton Library.
13. For further details about Nowell's vital spirit in her last months of life, see Elizabeth Evans, "Wolfe's Final Days: The Correspondence of Elizabeth Nowell and Annie Laurie Crawford," *Thomas Wolfe Newsletter* (Fall 1980), pp. 1–14.

A Note on the Text

The letters of Thomas Wolfe to Elizabeth Nowell are in the Thomas Wolfe Collection of William B. Wisdom, Houghton Library, Harvard University, Cambridge, Massachusetts, except for the letter of July 16, 1937, and the fragment from July 1937, both of which are in the North Carolina Collection, University of North Carolina Library, Chapel Hill, North Carolina. Half of them have been previously published in *The Letters of Thomas Wolfe*, edited by Elizabeth Nowell (Charles Scribner's Sons, 1956), although many paragraphs and sentences were omitted from them: February 2, 1934, pp. 401–3; April 23, 1935, pp. 457–58; September 8, 1936, p. 541 (postcard); September 14, 1936, p. 541 (postcard); January 24, 1937, pp. 603–4; undated, July 1937, pp. 635–38; July 29, 1937, pp. 647–48; undated fragment, pp. 651–54; December 29, 1937, pp. 695–96; May 3, 1938, pp. 750–52; May 12, 1938, pp. 763–64; May 23, 1938, pp. 766–67; May 26, 1938, p. 767; June 7, 1938, p. 768; June 15, 1938, pp. 769–70; June 19, 1938, pp. 770–72; June 20, 1938, p. 772 (postcard); June 22, 1938, p. 772 (postcard); June 29, 1938, p. 773; July 3, 1938, pp. 774–75. Complete texts of all the letters are printed in the present edition.

Most of the letters of Elizabeth Nowell to Thomas Wolfe are also in the Wisdom Collection. Those that are dated after May 11, 1938, and those dated July 19 and August 16, 18, 23, 1937, are in the North Carolina Collection, University of North Carolina Library. Her letters are here published for the first time, although I have omitted a few that dealt with unimportant business matters or went into complex detail about contracts for translation of Wolfe's books into foreign languages.

Because Elizabeth Nowell dashed off her letters hastily on the typewriter and because Wolfe frequently dictated his letters to a typist (and for some letters only the uncorrected carbon copies remain), I have corrected spelling and typographical errors and supplied some punctuation and paragraphing where needed for clarity and readability.

The text of "No More Rivers," which is published here for the first time, follows Wolfe's revised version in the Wisdom Collection at the Houghton Library. That copy has marks and notations in the margins by Elizabeth Nowell and by Helen McAfee of the *Yale Review*. I have adopted the punctuation, capitalization, and minor editorial adjustments that they agreed on but have not made any other changes that were requested by Helen McAfee.

Beyond Love and Loyalty

PART I 🌼 1934
Wolfe and the Maxim Lieber Agency

At the time this correspondence begins, Thomas Wolfe was acknowl-
edged to be one of the most promising novelists of his time. In 1929
he had published Look Homeward, Angel, *an autobiographical*
novel about the early years of a young man named Eugene Gant
growing up in a small Southern city in the Appalachians, and after
a Guggenheim fellowship had allowed him a year free of financial
worry, he had published three short novels in Scribner's Magazine,
"A Portrait of Bascom Hawke," "The Web of Earth," and "No
Door" (really a five-section sample of "work in progress" from his
second novel). He was running out of money by 1933, having used
up the generous advance on royalties that Charles Scribner's Sons
had given him for his next novel, and he needed an agent who could
help him sell some of his shorter episodes in the lucrative periodi-
cal market. His editor, Maxwell Perkins, recommended Elizabeth
Nowell, a former member of the Scribner staff, who was now work-
ing at the Maxim Lieber agency.

   The first piece that Wolfe sent to her was "Boom Town," a short
novel about a young man returning to his home in the South, stirred
by the memories it evoked but appalled by the changes that specu-
lation in real estate had brought about in the people.

🌼   🌼   🌼   Maxim Lieber
                      545 Fifth Avenue
                      New York City
                      December 1, 1933

Dear Mr. Wolfe:

   Here is your copy of Boom Town.[1] I think it's swell, and hope you
and Mr. Perkins[2] will too. There are a few more persnickety changes
that Lieber and I thought of for the last ten pages we did when we
were all so exhausted. They are so slight that we've sent the manuscript to Cosmopolitan today as planned, but some time after you've
read this over we might have one more session to discuss it. How
would next Wednesday night do? I promise you it'll be a very short
and peaceful session.

I hope you had a swell time on your week-end and are all rested up so you can sweep on with your book. We'll try to leave you in peace for a while now, but any time you want to bring the other stories over I'd love to start reading them.

Yours for bigger and
better markets,
Elizabeth Nowell

1. Published in the *American Mercury*, May 1934.
2. Maxwell Perkins, senior editor of Charles Scribner's Sons, Wolfe's publisher.

Maxim Lieber
545 Fifth Avenue
New York City
December 15, 1933

Dear Mr. Wolfe:

Here are some voluminous reactions to "In the Park." I hope they won't drive you wild and that you'll agree more or less. I'm not mailing the story because I think you said you had another copy and I didn't want it floating around in the undependable Christmas mails too much. Whether you agree more, less, or not at all I hope you'll give us a ring when you feel like it and hash it all over with us some night.

Yours
Maxim Lieber
Elizabeth Nowell
Committee for the Torture
of Authors

In the Park[1]

There are three reasons why I'm enthusiastic about your doing something with this: First, because it really has the feeling of that time—the "New York was awfully nice in those days" feeling. I think you could sharpen that up in spots but it's there anyway, in the descriptions and the quality of it, and in the gaiety and naivete of the way the people talked and acted. I think that feeling also has elements of popular appeal because God knows everybody loves the dear dead days. Secondly, people are always saying that you can't write about anything except what has actually happened to you in the past, and I'd just like to show them . . . And thirdly, this is short and consequently more saleable than a long story, so—

However, I may as well burst into the old refrain now as later. As it stands it is a narrative or a reminiscence and not what our friends the editors call a story. The more we can center it on the automobile idea the better the chances will be for selling it and the better the price, so I hope you won't mind too much if we harp continuously on that.

Therefore, what I wish you'd do—roughly and open to discussion —is this:

Plant the automobile idea in the first page by having the girl and her father see one as they walk up Broadway. Otherwise leave the first page up to the stars on page 2 mostly as it is, with maybe a little more heightening of the description. For instance, did the theatres have electric lights outside them or what in those days, and maybe could you suggest in just a couple of phrases what beautiful women were like because it seems to me that they were beautiful differently and dressed differently from any other time. Otherwise swell, up to the two priests, except that I wonder if a young girl of that era would say "God" so much???

I think the part about the two priests should be cut and sharpened somewhat. I wish you'd leave out the part about going to the convent which, believe it or not, is digression and doesn't help any despite its indisputable charm. I think it would help if the girl and her father went to White's and met the priests there and the conversation between them took place actually on that night instead of being vaguely remembered as having once occurred. I also think you could do just a speck more with the look and feeling of the restaurant, like that paragraph in the long piece about the train you left with me where you say "in great restaurants the light was brighter gold, but full and round like warm onyx columns, smooth warmly tinted marble, old wine in dark rounded age-encrusted bottles, and the great blonde figures of naked women on rose clouded ceilings." Maybe that wouldn't be true of White's but I bet Mr. Chapin would remember what it looked like enough for you to get a couple of sentences out of it, or I could try to find some pictures of it. I mean briefly, of course, or the automobile will get lost in the excitement.

Then have Mr. Gates come in, etc. etc., as is except for leaving out the little scattered reminiscences here and there like the part about his wife and his collection of Japanese curios[2] maybe. I don't think the driver should get so drunk that he couldn't even walk because that made me keep wondering how he was able to drive the car so well and why the girl wasn't more nervous, even if she was naive and of the pre-prohibition era. I also think you could put in a few more sentences telling how they actually started and describing the first thrill the girl got to be driving up there in the front seat so fast. The part about the policeman is *swell* and the sort of thing we want to stress most.

It is about the end that the real argument will begin. It seems to us that the automobile fades away too much in the excitement about the dawn and the birds and everything. Scribner's and Harper's would probably disregard this for the sake of all the other good qualities, but still we'd *much* rather it ended on a more definite note. Perhaps having the car break down and be towed by a horse is too banal, but couldn't it just break down and leave them sitting there waiting for a carriage to come along and take them home. While they were waiting they could hear the birds and be so thrilled that they didn't mind just sitting there, but finally they could hear a horse clopping along and the driver could pull up and take them in and vent some more disgust for those new-fangled cars, and let it end on that note more or less. Or maybe you'll have some other much better idea how to end it, but please end it with the automobile????

Yours
Miss Nowell and Lieber

1. Published in *Harper's Bazaar*, June 1935, and included later in *From Death to Morning*. The speaker in this story, Esther Jack, reminisces about a time in the early 1900s when she went out with her father to a fine restaurant and then for a ride in an automobile through Central Park.

2. The omission of the reference to the convent and to the Japanese curios are the only two suggestions that Wolfe accepted.

Maxim Lieber
545 Fifth Avenue
New York City
January 31, 1934

Dear Mr. Wolfe:

I've been trying to leave you in peace but the time now seems ripe to burst in where the angels fear to tread so I hope you and Perkins will forgive me.

First of all, about "Boom Town." We've been bickering with Harper's about it for almost a month and have finally had to accept defeat at their hands. After reading it twice they finally said they might take it with certain cuts which they specified, so we tried cutting it and showing them the result on the understanding that your approval would have to be obtained. We didn't want to bother you and take you away from the book until we were sure they would take it, which they've finally decided that they can't do. The reason I'm writing you now is that we think this shorter version is better and infinitely more saleable. The various people who saw the first version all complained about its length and also about the stuttering brother whose presence they couldn't understand. Of course in a book he would work in all right, but I do agree with the editor's complaint that in this he's too much of a shock and bound to take away the emphasis from the real estate theme. Of course too there's the old taboo about stuttering planted firmly in editor's minds because they think it slows up the reading too much, but the chief trouble is that Lee overshadows the boom theme. Anyway, instead of going into more explanations, I'm enclosing a copy of the new shorter version so you can see what you think of it. If you think it's all right we want to keep on trying the other magazines with it instead of the longer version.

In the meanwhile, Gringrich, the editor of that new man's magazine in Chicago, "Esquire," came in to see Lieber and said he was anxious to have something from you. He practically promised to take anything at all possible and to pay $175 for it which is $75 above his usual rate. The catch is that he can't use anything over 3000 words. I've been wondering if you'd want to try him with the part of "Morning in the City" about the man getting up.[1] There really isn't a chance in the world of selling the four parts complete and it seems as if this would be ideal for Esquire because it would be looked askance at by the more prudish magazines like Harper's, Atlantic, and the mass periodicals. It would have to have an ending tacked on to it to be a real story, but I wonder if you couldn't think of some kind of catastrophe that could happen to the man to round it out and to break off all his luxury and power with one short, sudden jolt. Perhaps he could find he'd lost his shirt in the Market, or was going to be called before the Senate Committee, or could get angina pectoris or something, but I mustn't let my imagination run away with me, especially when yours can run so much farther, faster, and better.

Anyway, we'll be looking forward to getting your reactions to both these situations when you get a chance to let us know. And I'm still hoping you'll do something with the automobile story sometime. I never thanked you for your Christmas card but I do now very much. I hope we can send you one for Easter or Valentine's or something in the form of a check for one thing or another.

Yours, Elizabeth Nowell

1. An early character sketch of Mr. Jack, which Wolfe later incorporated into "The Party at Jack's."

🌷 🌷 🌷   February 2, 1934
[carbon copy]
Dear Miss Nowell:

Thanks for your letter and for the revised copy of "Boom Town." I have not been able to read your revision carefully yet, but I shall read it over the week-end.

I am sorry you have had to work so hard on this and have had no better luck placing it. Of course there's no use arguing with Editors who know what they want or think they do, and I don't know of anything I can do to free them from their quaint superstitions concerning characters who stammer, etc. This was surprising news to me, and now I can no longer pretend even to guess at these prejudices or know what the next will be.

Frankly, I don't see that we can do very much more with this story, and it would seem to me to be the wiser course to let it drop. I have been very hard up and badly in need of money, but as much as I need and want it, it has never yet occurred to me that I could do honest work by carving, shaping, trimming, and finally by changing the entire structure and quality of a fundamental character. I think if I knew how to do it and understood more about the mysteries of magazine publishing, I would be tempted to go ahead and try to do it in order to get a little needed money, but I don't know how to do it, and I know nothing of these mysteries. It seems to me that it would be foolish for me to try to do something I do not understand.

One thing in your letter does surprise me, and that is that you now agree with the Editor's complaint that the character of "Lee" comes as too much of a shock in the story, that he overshadows the boom theme and takes away from the emphasis. My understanding at the beginning was that both you and Mr. Lieber liked the character of "Lee," felt definitely that he had a place in the story, and even thought that the character should be more fully developed and given a more important place which, as you remember, is exactly what we did in the revision.

I know you understand, Miss Nowell, that I am not quarreling with you about this, and that I do appreciate the pains you and Lieber have taken with this story. I am genuinely sorry not only for my sake but for yours that we are not likely now to get anything out of the work we've put into it. Moreover, I also believe that as a result of your comments and suggestions, I was able to make the piece more effective and interesting than it was in the beginning; and, of course, in the end that will always be a gain. But I do think that after we have talked and argued together about a piece we ought to come to some fairly definite agreement or conclusion about it, and that we can't go jumping around like a Jack-in-the box changing our minds and opinions every time we come up against a new Editor.

I am very grateful to you for all the extra work you've gone to on your own hook in making this new revision and shortening the piece and cutting out "Lee's" stammering; but it seems fairly evident to me now that the piece is not commercially saleable, and I doubt that we are going to have any success with it. But I will read your copy over carefully Sunday, and either call or write you about it next week.

Now about the Esquire proposition. I think something can be done about this, and if you can get $175 that will be swell. I have been talking to Mr. Perkins about it, and he has suggested two or three short pieces which are either in the manuscript of the book or have been cut out of it. One is a piece about two boys going down to see a big circus come into town, unload, and put up the tents in the early morning.[1] I think I will send you this piece today or tomorrow. It is out of the book and in its present form is only seven typed pages long, or about 2100 words. The thing needs an introduction which I will try to write today, but otherwise it is complete enough, although, again, I am afraid it is not what most people consider a story.

I also have what Max calls one of my "dithyrambs." He and Dashiell[2] are very kind about it, and Dashiell even suggested it might be used for the magazine, but I sold them another story the other day, which makes three they have taken recently, so I don't know whether they would care to use it. The thing is about the names of America—the names of rivers, the tramps, the railroads, the states, the Indian Tribes, etc.[3] The only story element in it is that it begins with four episodes in dialogue of different people abroad who are thinking of home. Perkins thinks this piece goes beyond the 3,000 word limit, but I believe it could be brought within that limit without much trouble. It is to start the seventh section of my book.

I also have a piece called "The Bums at Sunset"[4] which we cut out of the book the other day, and which is about some hoboes waiting beside the track to pick up the train, but I don't know if this is any good or could be used.

There are a great number of these pieces, and I think you might very probably find something among them that you could use, but I have lost confidence in my own powers of selection, and apparently have little idea which part of my writing is going to please people and what they're going to like. The piece about the names of America I wrote two or three years ago, and I'm almost positive I showed it to Mr. Perkins, but he says now he never saw it before and that it is one of the best things I ever wrote. In the same way he says that a section of 20,000 words or so which was cut out of one of the stories that the magazine published last summer is a fine story and some of the best writing I ever did, and that he never saw it before. So I revised it and fixed it up at his suggestion and I suppose they have taken it.

All I can do now and what I am doing in addition to revising and re-writing the book is to get all of these things typed so that he can read them. If I had time I'd ask you to go over my manuscript with me, but I haven't got the time because I am meeting Mr. Perkins every day now to work on the book, and all the rest of the time I spend in writing and in getting the manuscript typed. But I'll send the circus piece to you and you can see if there is any chance of doing anything with the Esquire people about it, and if you don't think there is, I'll send you something else.

If and when I get through with this enormous manuscript, I have a number of short pieces that I want to write, and maybe then I can really give you something that you can sell.

This is all for the present. Try to sell something to Esquire if you can. I do need the money badly.

Sincerely,

1. Published as "Circus at Dawn" in *Modern Monthly*, April 1935, and later included in *From Death to Morning*.

2. Alfred "Fritz" Dashiell, the editor of *Scribner's Magazine*.

3. Published as "The Names of the Nation" in *Modern Monthly*, December 1934.

4. Published in *Vanity Fair*, October 1935, and later included in *From Death to Morning*.

❧ ❧ ❧   March 8, 1934

[carbon copy]
Mr. Maxim Lieber
545 Fifth Avenue
New York City
Dear Lieber:

Thanks for your note and for the enclosed check representing my share of the sale of *Boom Town* to the *American Mercury*. It is certainly a welcome addition to my lean and hungry pocket book, and although I hoped we would get more for all the work we did, I am glad we got something and I hope we both have even better luck next time.

This is all for the present.

I shall meet you at your office Friday night about seven-fifteen.

Sincerely yours,
[Thomas Wolfe]

❦ ❦ ❦   Maxim Lieber
                          545 Fifth Avenue
                          New York City
                          June 1, 1934

Dear Mr. Wolfe:

As you will see by the enclosed, Hansen[1] wants to nominate *Boom Town* for inclusion in the O. Henry memorial collection of short stories. It isn't exactly sewed up yet because after he gets your promise he has to submit it to the approval of the other judges. If they agree with him that means that it goes into the book and has a chance to get the prize for the long short story. They do not pay anything for using it in the book, if they do use it, but hold out the glittering possibility of the first prize, which, as I remember it, is $500. So the thing for you to do if you like the idea, is to give Hansen permission to enter *Boom Town* and then keep your fingers crossed. I am also enclosing a couple of clippings which the Mercury sent me from two Southern newspapers, and I hope all of this will make you feel better and not so much inclined to believe that those couple of "stuffed shirt" friends of Dashiell's were right in not liking the story. I also hope that everything else is O.K. again with you.

                          Yours, Nowell

1. Harry Hansen later included "Boom Town" in O. *Henry Memorial Award: Prize Stories of 1934.*

❦ ❦ ❦   June 2, 1934

Dear Miss Nowell:

Thanks for your letter and the enclosed noted from Hansen. I have just written him telling him he could enter "Boom Town" in the O. Henry contest, and perhaps unwisely but scrupulously I also told him that some of the material for the story had been taken out of a book and would again be used in a book some day. But I don't think he should object to this since I explained that the whole thing has been re-written and re-shaped to story form. Anyway, thanks for your interest and here's hoping for the best.

I am now working afternoon and night. I can't honestly say I do much mornings. Mr. Perkins and I are working together at night from eight-thirty on. I am putting a great deal in and he is taking a great deal out, but so far I can hardly call it a draw.[1]

I have been thinking of asking you if you would call in anything of mine which you have sent out. I don't think it is a good thing to send those pieces around any longer. I want to try again with something new and I hope with more chance of acceptance, but it is not going to do me any good at present to have this stuff passed around and sent back, so please get it back for me, and as soon as I get something new that looks possible, I'll send it to you. I am feeling O.K. again and working my head off. My English publisher,[2] by the way, wrote and told me that he had sold one of my stories—"The Sun and the Rain"—to *Nash's Magazine* in England. He says they are paying twenty guineas for it. I haven't figured that out yet, but it's better than a kick in the eye.

I saw our patient[3] for the last time and maybe, alas, forever the night before he left the krankenhaus. By that time I, too, had been admitted to the rapidly growing circles of the damned. I still fail to see just where and how I wronged him. All I did was to let him have a little money, about as much as I could afford, and go to see him four or five times a week and telephone to people about his dire need and try to sell a story. Fritz Dashiell finally turned down the story. It is true I delayed a day in telling Francis because I fell asleep after working and didn't get to the hospital in time. He seemed to want to make an issue over it and implied that because of the day's delay I had prevented him from doing this or that or something really constructive. I don't think I did, but let him have it that way if he wants to. Anyway, that makes everyone a bum now. I hope he sells his stories or that you will sell one for him because that may help him to see things a little more calmly.

This is all for the present. Do as I ask you to do, please, about getting my stuff back for me, and I'll try to give you something else as soon as anything looks hopeful. Meanwhile, with best wishes,

Sincerely yours,

P.S. Thanks for the clippings about "Boom Town," but I made the front page and got three columns in the Asheville paper. They quoted a large part of the story verbatim. I don't know what the result was, but I should think that the *Mercury* might have a good sale there.

1. Perkins was working with Wolfe every evening helping him to cut and reorganize *Of Time and the River*.

2. A. S. Frere-Reeves of William Heinemann Ltd.

3. Owen Francis, a young writer from the South whom Wolfe had attempted to help.

June 18th, 1934
5 Montague Terrace
[carbon copy]   Brooklyn, N.Y.
Miss Elizabeth Nowell
c/o Maxim Lieber
545 5th Avenue
New York City, N.Y.
Dear Miss Nowell:

I wrote you on June second and asked you to get me all of my manuscript which you had in your office or had sent out. So far, I have had no answer from you and I am writing again to remind you of my former letter and to ask you again to get the manuscript for me.

As I told you in my previous letter, I don't want that manuscript sent out any longer. If and when I publish another book should there be any demand for what I do, I should be glad to have you try again, but at the present time I feel that it does more harm than good, and I, therefore, ask you again and depend on you to see to it that none of this stuff is shown around any more.

Please let me hear from you at once about the manuscript.

Meanwhile, with best wishes,

Sincerely yours,

Maxim Lieber
545 Fifth Avenue
New York City
June 21, 1934
Dear Mr. Wolfe:

Here alas and at last are the stories back as you asked. There is no sense in saying how sorry I am or anything, so I'll just say I hope we'll have better luck another time when things aren't so hectic.

I'm enclosing some of the letters that we got from magazines. Unfortunately the ones from the Atlantic were written in a very personal long-hand scrawl by a friend of mine up there and I didn't bother to file them. The Harper reactions were by word of mouth in several sessions so I haven't anything on that either. I'm sorry.

Yours, Nowell

❦ ❦ ❦   Maxim Lieber
                                     545 Fifth Avenue
                                     New York City
                                     June 29, 1934

Dear Mr. Wolfe:

Cheer up, the O. Henry anthology definitely wants to use BOOM TOWN. I've just had a phone [call] from Harry Hansen's secretary asking for a biographical note about you, and since I'm not sure of all the details I wonder if you can get Miss what's-her-name to send me all the dope. If that's too much trouble I'll try to get it from Scribner's but Will Weber is on his vacation and I hate to bother Mr. Perkins.

                                     Yours, Nowell

❦ ❦ ❦   No. 5 Montague Terrace
                                     Brooklyn, New York
                                     June 30, 1934

Miss Elizabeth Nowell
Care of Maxim Lieber
545 Fifth Avenue
New York, N.Y.

Dear Miss Nowell:

Thanks for your note. I am glad to know Hansen wants "Boom Town" for the O. Henry anthology, and hope we get something out of it besides cloying honor! As for the biographical note, I suppose this is what you want:

The whole name is Thomas Clayton.

Thirty-three years old.

Born Asheville, North Carolina.

Was graduated from the University of North Carolina in 1920. Went to Harvard for three years—1920–1923—and got Master's Degree there in 1922.

Was instructor in English at the Washington Square College of New York University for four years between 1924 and 1930, and spent the rest of that time abroad.

Published "Look Homeward, Angel," 1929.

Went abroad, 1930, on a Guggenheim Fellowship and came back in 1931.

Since that time have lived in Brooklyn, published some stories— all in Scribner's Magazine except for "Boom Town"—and worked on the manuscript of the series of books to be known by the general title of "Time and the River."

I believe this is all. I have tried to make it as short as possible, but if not short enough, you do the rest.

It was too bad about the Red Book.[1] I was hoping that they could see their way clear to publish the story a month or two earlier, and it was hard to have to pass the money up, because as you know, it would be extremely welcome at the present time. But I do also see Mr. Perkin's "pernt." He does feel quite strongly that the book should not be delayed any longer than possible for any reason, and no matter when it does come out, I am confident he wants to get it in the hands of the printer at the earliest possible time.

Again, thanks to you for continuing to take an interest and to push my wares after so many disappointments. Maybe we will both have better luck some day, and I really think we shall.

Meanwhile, with best wishes again,

> Sincerely yours,
> Tom Wolfe

1. Nowell had sold an excerpt from "Telemachus," Part 2 of *Of Time and the River*, to *Redbook* for $750, but because the editors could not print the story before the scheduled publication of the complete novel, it had to be withdrawn. It concerned Eugene Gant's misadventures on an automobile trip to South Carolina that led to his being put in jail.

PART II ❧ February to July 1935
Nowell Begins Her Own Agency

By early 1935, Wolfe had completed his second novel, Of Time and
the River, *the further adventures of Eugene Gant as he aspired to
become a playwright at Harvard University, as he became over-
whelmed by the heterogeneity of city life that he found in Boston and
New York, and as he sought to satisfy his cultural hunger in England
and France, only to discover an intense awareness of his American
heritage.*

*Just before the book was published, Wolfe sailed to Europe for a
vacation. But before he departed, he gave Elizabeth Nowell, who
had now established her own literary agency, the entire bulk of his
accumulated manuscript, episodes that had been cut from* Of Time
and the River *or were parts of the Eugene Gant cycle yet to come.
She was to hunt through that material on the lookout for short
publishable items. As it turned out, the literary excitement over* Of
Time and the River *made it easier for her to place Wolfe's work with
magazine editors than she had been able to do in earlier months.*

❧ ❧ ❧   5 Montague Terrace
                 Brooklyn
                 [February 1935]
Dear Miss Nowell:
    I am glad to hear that you are starting a literary agency on your
own account and I am writing to tell you that I should be pleased if
you will continue to act as my agent for any manuscripts of mine
for which you may be able to find a market on the usual 10%
commission basis.
                          Sincerely yours,
                          Thomas Wolfe

❦ ❦ ❦   Charles Scribners Sons
                                 597 Fifth Avenue
                                 New York
                                 February 9, 1935
Dear Miss Nowell:
   I hereby authorize you to act as my agent with respect to the
moving picture rights to my novel, "Of Time and the River."
                                 Sincerely yours,
                                 Thomas Wolfe

❦ ❦ ❦   Elizabeth Nowell
                                 114 East 56th Street
                                 New York
                                 March 1, 1935
Dear Mr. Wolfe:
   I called up the Lexington to say good-bye to you, but I guess you'd
already gone to meet Mrs. J.[1] in your soup-and-fish and undershirt.
So I'm writing this instead because I know you'll be too hectic for
telephone calls in the morning, and there'll probably be so many
people milling around at the dock that I'd only add to the confusion by offering to help, (although if you want me to be sure to
phone me).
   Don't worry about anything because Mr. Perkins and I will work
on things together while you're gone, and have the swellest trip ever,
and a good rest and all the luck in the world. That is, if you want to
call it luck, although of course it isn't that so much as what goes on
inside that head of yours. Anyway, call it whatever you want, I know
you'll have plenty of "money of your own" when you come back and
have the keys to the city and everything else. Yea, verily, even Hervey
Allen[2] will bend the knee as you step ashore.
   All fooling aside, though, I want to try to say how much I think of
your work. Perkins was taking me to task the other day for never
having expressed anything near the admiration I've got for the book,
or the coming books, or anything you do as far as that goes. I guess
he was teasing me more or less, but it did hurt my feelings because I
always took it for granted you and he knew how I felt. Maybe I've
some kind of a Yankee repression, but goddamn it you must know
about it whether I show it by sitting up all night working with you or
by raving around like most of these other fool women. I can't help
feeling self-conscious even now, and imagining your showing this to

him the way you did Miss Beam's.[3] But you know I know you've got more talent and poetry and sincerity and greatness in your little finger than all the other writers I can think of put together. It's fallen on me to pick on you about all the nasty little details that magazine editors carp at, and I'm afraid you'll always think of me as dragging you out of the Chatham bar or waving a blue pencil in your face. But underneath all that I always get a tremendous inspiration out of your things and out of working with you. Well, you must realize that if you stop to think about it. And I guess you realize too how grateful I am at the way you stuck with me and helped me these last two months. Maybe this still sounds New England-frost-bound or whatever you call it, but I've got tears in my eyes writing it, and I'll keep on showing how much I do feel by working like hell on everything I can while you're away.

Yours, Nowell

1. Belinda Jelliffe, the wife of the psychoanalyst, Dr. Smith Ely Jelliffe.
2. Hervey Allen's novel, *Anthony Adverse*, an international bestseller, was widely admired at the time.
3. Gwenyth Beam, a secretary in the Scribner office who had typewritten a good deal of Wolfe's manuscript.

 Mar. 1, 1935

DEAR MISS NOWELL THANKS FOR YOUR FINE LETTER I SHALL ALWAYS VALUE AND REMEMBER WHAT YOU SAID AND I SEND YOU GRATEFUL THANKS FOR YOUR FRIENDSHIP AND LOYAL AND DEVOTED SERVICE FOR WHICH I HOPE YOU WILL SOME DAY RECEIVE ADEQUATE REWARD HOPE TO SEE YOU AGAIN IN MAY BEST WISHES
THOMAS WOLFE

114 East 56th Street
New York
March 22, 1935

Dear Mr. Wolfe:

This is just to keep the record straight in your absence. I have sold your story "Gulliver"[1] to Scribner's Magazine for $200, and have sent Mr. Perkins, as your temporary representative, a check for $180 (200 minus my regular agent's commission of 10%). Since you have no bank, as I understand from Mr. Perkins, he is crediting this $180 to your royalty account with Charles Scribner's Sons.

I have also sold "In the Park" to Harper's Bazaar for $300. Their check has not come through as yet, but I shall be sending Perkins $270 in payment for that story in a few days.

Sincerely yours,
Elizabeth Nowell

1. Published in *Scribner's Magazine*, June 1935, and later included in *From Death to Morning*.

❧ ❧ ❧

St. George's Court
26, Hanover Square, W.I.
[postmarked April 23, 1935]
Easter Monday! and how!—
when they have Easter here it
lasts four days—Sunday all
the time.

Dear Miss Nowell:

I've been very bad about writing you—wanted to a dozen times—but so damned tired and nervous when I got over here that I didn't write anyone for several weeks—and now just time for a note to you —I'm leaving London today after being here a month—going up to Norfolk for a few days and then to Germany via Harwich and Hook of Holland. My German publisher[1] has wired saying he wants my book and for me to come on over and will pay expenses but coyly refrains from mentioning terms—I understand, however, that whatever money I get from Germans will have to be spent there in the country—so it looks as if I'll have to go there and live riotously for a week or two or get nothing at all. I have a most humorous plan whereby I'll use Herr Hitler's currency to pay the expenses of a trip to Russia, but friends here say they think I'll strike a snag—anyway there's no harm trying—have had little news from U.S.A. save letters and two cables from Max Perkins, but heard indirectly (through letter Max wrote to Frere Reeves my English publisher) that "Tom's agent has sold four stories"—Darling, I am torn between joy and trepidation; the news if true is swell but I don't know where the hell you *found* the four stories—if one of them is about *Pett* and the orphan girl[2] for God's sake try to change the names and the locale if possible—anyway, upon the strength of rumor, counting my chickens before I've seen them, and my princely hypothetical wealth, I've gone and had several suits of clothes made by the Prince of Wales own royally-appointed pantsmaker, and am now the damnedest fop and triple-gazzaza dude that American literature has ever known—so for God's sake, don't tell me when I get back home it ain't true!—

I have begun to perk up recently, am eating and sleeping with considerable regularity—something I had not accomplished often in recent years—and if all goes for the best I may in time succeed in recovering a portion of my ravaged vitality and my wasted youth—hope this finds you well and not staying up nights writing stories for the ungrateful authors—take care of yourself, and since I'm wishing *you* good luck, why good luck to *both* of us. Will see you, I hope, in May—

Wolfe

1. Ernst Rowohlt of Rowohlt Verlag, Berlin.

2. A section that had been cut from *Look Homeward, Angel* and that referred clearly to Wolfe's aunt, "Pett" Westall. In a revised form, it became Chapter 5 of *The Web and the Rock*.

114 East 56th Street
New York
May 6, 1935

Dear Wolfe:

Bless your heart and don't worry any more because Pett's story isn't one of the four sold. I asked Mr. Perkins a couple of times if I couldn't write you yet but he always drew down his granite brows without saying anything, and it was only last week that he finally admitted that there was no reason why I shouldn't. Then he went to Baltimore for a few days (May 1 is the time you start getting inoculated for hay fever), and your letter came while he was still away. Anyway, I've been wanting to write you ever since you sent me that night letter before you sailed, and if I didn't it was because I knew what Perkins meant and I didn't want to be a pest but to give you all the rest and peace you could get. I've been thinking of things to tell you ever since—about all the excitement over the book and everything—but if I try to put them all down this will be the world's longest letter. I kept wishing you were here to realize all the real recognition you'd finally got because you'll probably never believe it just reading about it but it even got me so excited that I was treading on air for a week or so, so God knows what it would have done to the actual recipient of all the praise. I guess that's the sort of thing I shouldn't write you too much of, but I can't help saying that I was with Perkins when he sent you that first cable and for an example of New England understatement and caution it wins first prize.[1] Maybe this sounds as if I was trying to criticize him but you know I'm not —just trying to explain how he took it all, cool as a cucumber but with his face all lit up that way and his eyes brighter than ever. You know.

As for the stories they're as follows: "In the Park" to Harper's Bazaar for $300, (and think of all the beautiful "dangerous women fans" you'll get from *that* magazine); "Arnold" to Esquire for $200, and "The Other Side of the House" to Cosmopolitan—1200 words for $350. The only thing I'm worried about is that Cosmo wanted to call it "The Cottage by the Track"[2] and after due deliberation with Perkins I told them all right, figuring you wouldn't mind so much prostituting your titles for 29¢ a word as for nothing in Calverton's[3] case. Also the editor of Esquire is named Arnold Gingrich so he is calling the story "Arnold Pentland" to be sure nobody gets him mixed up with it. When your letter came I got a horrible sinking feeling that maybe you'd forgotten and used Arnold's real name, meaning to change it later. So I made Terry wire your mother to be sure and she wired back that Bascom's[4] sons were named Harold and Carl, and now I've [written] her to explain so she won't worry about anything's being printed to raise any trouble. I had to cut out the daughter to get it down to Esquire length (4000 about) and Arnold comes out as pretty likeable and pathetic all the way around.

The money for the stories I turned over to Perkins P.D.Q. to avoid pulling a Boyd on you,[5] and he deposited it to your account with Scribner's. I asked him if we couldn't put it in a bank so you'd have "money of your own" but he didn't feel that he had the authority or something, though he says you can draw the whole works out when you come back and put it in a bank yourself so you won't have to beg Cross[6] for any measly little $15 bits of it. Cosmo's check isn't due till this week but the rest is all salted down at Scribner's with letters telling you just how much was deposited being held there so there'll be a complete record.

Perkins let me copy out "Only the Dead Know Brooklyn"[7] and I think Mercury may take it—will know in a few days. But I'm not going to meddle with anything else from October Fair because it's mostly so personal and I know you wouldn't want me to go rushing ahead without your full authorization. Palmer,[8] the new Mercury editor, is full of ideas and wanted me to ask you to write a story of a Rhodes scholar from start to finish. But I strongly advise you not to. He wouldn't give me a definite commission for you and God knows we don't want to go doing any more things on "speculation." And you write just whatever you damn please and to hell with all bright editorial ideas. So just forget it, I would. If you ever do write the story about the young men who died the same year as Ben[9] or about Bermuda[10] or any of those send them over and I'll type them out or hire somebody to anyway and I think we can sell them. (That crossed out place said "cut them down," just taking it for granted! and I apologize.) But I know you're too busy drinking in everything new you see so I guess you'll do better by saving the actual writing till you get back. But I know you know all that anyway.

As for the preface that they didn't use I think we'll have to wait till you get back for that because "The Artist in America" doesn't hitch on to the other part quite right. I wrote your friend Mr. Sanderson Vanderbilt[11] a very stern letter which scared the life out of him—saying that I understood you had lent him a portion of your manuscript and would he kindly return it since it was desired for publication. Well, he found it and sent it back after turning the whole Herald-Tribune inside out and we had innumerable long telephone calls in which I told him what I thought of that interview and he was abject as hell and made me promise to apologize to you and Perkins and to ask the latter for a chance to make good sometime. He told me that his own mother had written him reproving him for looking at your unpaid bills etc. etc. and he was a pretty cowed and repentant guy all around.

I've sent copies of the four stories to Pollinger of Curtis Brown[12] to sell in England, so if you're going back there and want to see "Arnold" and "Gulliver" in their final forms he's a nice guy and I know he'd like to meet you. (6 Henrietta St. Covent Garden.) but of course there's no real need if you don't want. I'm just telling you so if any English editor says he saw a story of yours you won't say "What story" in horror.

As for the German edition of the book I'm not trying to butt in or anything, and I hope to God that it's all settled and everything [is] rosey by the time this letter reaches you. But if you think they're trying to railroad you into unfair terms or anything you let the thing ride. E. P. Tal and Co Verlag, which is about the biggest and best publisher in Vienna, wrote asking for a chance at the German language rights and I wrote them that Rowohlt had an option and they replied as per enclosed card. (You can have only one German language edition, either in Germany proper, Austria, or Switzerland.) France, Italy, all three Scandinavian countries, Czechoslovakia, Holland, Spain are now considering copies and I've written and sent reviews to Brazil (Portuguese rights) and Jugoslavia. Oh yes, and I wrote John Cudahy, who is the U.S. Ambassador to Poland, to ask him what he knew about publishing you in Poland maybe. He's sort of an amateur writer himself and used to be more or less of a beau of mine, so if you get in any difficulties about changing marks to roubles or anything or if you pass through Warsaw you could tell him that I'd written you about him.

I guess this is the most important stuff, tho there's a lot of little incidents and things. Terry and I are thick as thieves and one of his young writers—Morris Tucker—I think is the real stuff, so maybe I can sell some things for him. Blythe's biography[13] turned out to have some swell stuff in it, but had no authentication and was just exactly twice too long. I wrote him a 19 page criticism which he's taken like a brave boy and is following, also providing notes and documentation and a preface by Henderson[14] or somebody. Perkins was wearing a very swell broad crocheted tie the last time I saw him—stripes in 3 lovely shades of grey to match his suit exactly. I couldn't help mentioning it and he gave me one of those beautiful sheepish smiles and said "Mrs. J. gave it to me." So maybe you'd better rush home to protect him. No more now, but have the swellest time in the world and a good rest and everything else like that, and *please* don't worry about anything because everything is 100% O.K.

                                                    Yrs   Nowell

1. Perkins's cable, "Magnificent reviews, somewhat critical in ways expected, full of greatest praise," did not convey the real literary excitement that reviewers displayed over *Of Time and the River*.

2. Published in *Cosmopolitan*, July 1935, and later included in *From Death to Morning*.

3. Nowell resented Wolfe's generosity to V. F. Calverton: Wolfe gave him pieces to publish in *Modern Monthly* that she could have sold to magazines.

4. Wolfe's uncle, Henry Westall, was the model for Uncle Bascom in *Of Time and the River*. His son, Harold, was the model for "Arnold." John Terry, an old friend of the Wolfe family, was at that time an assistant professor of English at New York University.

5. Madeleine Boyd, who had been Wolfe's first literary agent, failed to give Wolfe the royalty advance she had received from Rowohlt Verlag for the publication of *Look Homeward, Angel*. When he discovered her mishandling of his money, Wolfe discharged her.

6. Robert Cross, head of the Scribner accounting department, who disliked Wolfe's practice of drawing upon his royalty account every few days for current living expenses: he felt that Wolfe was calling upon the publishing house to render banking services.

7. Published in the *New Yorker*, June 15, 1935, and later included in *From Death to Morning*.

8. Paul Palmer.

9. Wolfe's brother, Ben, had died during the influenza epidemic of 1918.

10. An unpublished sketch entitled "The Still Vex'd Bermoothes."

11. Vanderbilt had behaved shabbily in his treatment of Wolfe in an interview published in the *New York Herald Tribune*, February 18, 1935. He had snooped about his apartment looking at his personal belongings and unpaid bills. Also Wolfe had given him an excerpt from the planned but unpublished preface to *Of Time and the River* about the problems of the American artist. Nowell had retrieved it from Vanderbilt when she was trying to salvage the rejected preface to sell as a literary essay by Wolfe.

12. Nowell used the London branch of the Curtis Brown literary agency for sale of Wolfe's work to British magazines.

13. LeGette Blythe's *Marshall Ney: A Dual Life* was eventually published in 1937. He and Wolfe had been college students together at the University of North Carolina.

14. Archibald Henderson, the biographer, who had been one of Wolfe's professors at the University of North Carolina.

114 East 56th Street
New York
May 31, 1935

Dear Wolfe:

Just a line in haste to say that the New Yorker has paid $275 for "Only the Dead Know Brooklyn" and I have sent Perkins my check for $248 which equals that sum minus my 10% commission.

There is also a small sum of about $3 due you in part payment for the German magazine rights to Boomtown which Frankfurter Zeitung bought through Lieber's agent. I shall send Perkins the check and the exact amount due and all the other details as soon as I get it straight from Lieber who merely says in his letter that it is a "partial payment" because the German government will allow only 10 R.M. a month to leave the country on one item.

Yrs   Nowell

114 East 56th Street
New York
June 6, 1935

Dear Wolfe:

This is to say that I have just sent Perkins my check for $3.53 which represents the first payment exported from Germany for the purchase of "Boom Town" by the Frankfurter Zeitung. The story was translated and sold by Dr. Hans Buetow who asked for the opportunity to do so through the Mercury. Augoff sent the request to me when I was still with Lieber and while I was sick the deal was concluded by Max. He (Max) has now sent me his check for $3.92 for this first payment, and he has deducted no commission but I have taken my 39¢.

The deal was as follows: Buetow was to receive half of the purchase price and you the other half, and the price was R.M. 220 which makes R.M. 110 for you. However the German embargo on money is such that only R.M. 10 can be sent you a month, and the $3.92 represents this first monthly instalment. Of course had I known about it you could have eaten and travelled on the 110 when you were there but Max didn't mention it till now.

Yours, Nowell

❧   ❧   ❧   114 East 56th Street
                                       New York
                                       June 27, 1935

Dear Wolfe:

I've just sent Perkins my check for $3.56 in payment of the second instalment due on the German price for Boom Town. Pretty small potatoes when it comes in little hunks like this, but anyway its deposited to your credit.

Yrs   Nowell

P.S. The O. Henry collection wanted to use "Only the Dead Know Brooklyn" so Perkins and I have given them our joint consent in your absence. Hope that's all right. I know you were a little sore at Hansen about something he said about "Boom Town" but he really meant terribly well and his review of "Of Time and the River" will convince you I guess.

❧   ❧   ❧   114 East 56th Street
                                       New York
                                       July 2, 1935

Dear Wolfe:

This is just to say welcome home at last, and to explain why I'm missing from the scene. I had to go home some time to see Mother about some things and I got four days vacation this time and on a special $10 round-trip ticket, so I figured I'd better go. Will be back late Sunday night and hope I see you whenever you get a chance next week, and will call up Mr. Perkins to find out where you are etc. etc. with that idea in mind. I guess you'll probably go somewhere with him over the fourth anyway and there'll be a million things you'll want to talk over with him before you even unpack your bag. Well, it certainly will be swell to see you again and hear all the latest and tell you just how all your foreign rights and things stand. There's a pile of notes I've written you from time to time waiting with this one;

just to be sure I itemize all your sales etc. but I guess it'll take a couple of weeks too to wade through all your fan mail. Take it easy anyway, and I'll be looking forward to seeing you.

Yrs   Nowell

P.S. One thing I forgot and that is Martha Foley and Whit Burnett[1] phoned me and said they were going to lecture in Colorado with you and would you want to plan to go out there with them. I said your plans were pretty hard to tell about and they'd better not pay any attention to you but they said to be sure and tell you in case you wanted to get in touch with them. Otherwise I don't think you have to bother about it at all.

EN

1. Husband and wife, who were the editors of *Story* magazine.

The following letter from Wolfe to his fellow novelist, Vardis Fisher, is included here because it is the only piece outside the Nowell correspondence that reveals how Wolfe really felt about his agent. Elizabeth Nowell, in an access of modesty, omitted this letter from her edition of The Letters of Thomas Wolfe.

Wolfe and Fisher were old friends: both had been instructors in English at New York University in the 1920s.

🌱 🌱 🌱   New York City, July 17, 1935

Dear Vardis:

I've wanted to write you for a long time—have been away in Europe for four months and just got back. For the last four years I haven't had time for much contemporary reading but I do want to tell you that I read *In Tragic Life* and I think it had some of the most powerful and magnificent writing that has been done in America in my years. I am writing you this to tell you so, and of how happy and glad I am to see evidence everywhere of your growing work and reputation, and I would like also here to recommend to you—if you ever need her services—a young lady who has labored valiantly and splendidly in my behalf as an agent.

I know you understand that I have absolutely no other motive—nothing to gain—by recommending this girl, except that she's far and away the best agent I ever knew, absolutely honest and reliable, is not out to make money for herself—believe it or not, this is true—and is genuinely interested in your work.

I took the liberty of giving her your name before I went to Europe and I believe she has written you. Anyway, her name is Elizabeth Nowell, she lives at 114 East 56th Street, New York City. She worked here on Scribner's Magazine for years, served a year's partnership with Maxim Lieber, a literary agent, and is now starting as an agent on her own hook. She has absolutely no connection with any of my books published by Scribner's, but she has done a good job placing the books in foreign countries, and while I was away she sold six stories for me, and has done many other things for me with great intelligence and good sense. —Further, I believe she will do far more for the people she represents than one of these big machine-like high pressure cyclones, and if you have any stories, articles, essays, or short pieces of any kind I know you could entrust them to her with complete confidence, and that she would do a good and faithful job. I certainly want to see her get some good people now, because she deserves it, and if you have anything to send to her, I wish you would.

This is all for the present. I've got to go out to Colorado next week and am looking forward to seeing some of the Great West I have dreamed about and wanted to see so much. I wish I could see you— I don't know if you're coming this way soon, but if you are here this autumn please look me up through Scribners. Good-bye, Vardis —I am so happy about your success and the growing power and substance of your work—I know you'll do it—

With every good wish and friendly greeting—
                                        Sincerely—
                                        Tom Wolfe.

Wolfe's Newly Acquired Fame

The next months of 1935 reflect some of the rewards that came to Wolfe as Of Time and the River *gained widespread critical recognition. When he traveled to Berlin to meet his German publisher, Ernst Rowohlt, who had just brought out* Look Homeward, Angel *in an excellent German translation, he was greeted as an international celebrity. In the summer he was invited to speak at the Colorado Writers Conference in Boulder, where he became the center of attention soon after he arrived. In his lecture he described the anguish he felt during his creative labors with* Of Time and the River *and the help he had received from Maxwell Perkins in giving the book its final shape, but he also communicated the intensity of his feeling about the American landscape and the vitality of the American people.*

Scribner's followed up the success of Of Time and the River *by issuing, in the fall of 1935, a collection of Wolfe's short fiction,* From Death to Morning. *Elizabeth Nowell then persuaded Wolfe to publish his Colorado lecture under the title "The Story of a Novel" in the* Saturday Review of Literature. *This account stirred up so much interest that Perkins decided to publish it in book form, using Wolfe's revised and extended version.*

As the letters indicate, this publication provided the occasion for the first and only quarrel that Wolfe had with Miss Nowell. After behaving meanly and insultingly about her request for a commission on the book, he later came to see that her claim was justified, and he humbled himself in an abject apology. Their relationship continued somewhat strengthened by the fact that they had weathered such a stormy episode. Wolfe learned to respect Miss Nowell even more as a result of her spunky self-defense during this trial of friendship.

❦ ❦ ❦   Denver, Colorado
                                                     August 14, 1935
Miss Elizabeth Nowell
114 East Fifty-Sixth Street
New York, New York
Dear Miss Nowell:

I am getting this letter off to you in a hurry because a newspaper man is on his way down here to interview me at the present moment, and these Denver people are running me ragged with their wonderful hospitality. I want to write you a more detailed letter later on, but at the present time all I can ask you to do is this:

Will you please telephone Mr. Cornelius Mitchell of the firm of Mitchell and Van Winkle, 350 Madison Avenue, as soon as you get this letter. He has written me an urgent letter by air mail asking me to try to locate, if possible, the letter Mrs. Boyd wrote me in answer to my letter dismissing her as my agent in 1932, and he has further asked me if I would get in touch with the Czechoslovakian publishers of my last book and try to secure, even if I have to cable for it, the original or a copy of Mrs. Boyd's recent correspondence with them in which she acknowledged that she had nothing to do with the second book.[1] I have just found Mr. Mitchell's letter, by the way, and the address of the Czechoslovakian firm is Sfinx Centrum, Smecky 2, Prague, Czechoslovakia. I believe, although I am not certain, that you have made arrangements with them already for the publication of "Of Time and the River." Anyway, will you please call Mr. Mitchell up at once and find out what he wants, and then if you think it possible to secure a copy of the correspondence, get hold of it by all means even if you have to cable. This is all for the present.

I am on my way to Santa Fe tomorrow and will be there until Saturday at least. You can reach me at the La Fonda Hotel, Santa Fe, New Mexico. I shall write you again from there and try to give you future mailing addresses.

I hope all is going well with you and that when I come back to New York early in September I will find you in good health and ready to help me again with your extremely valuable and appreciated services.

I had a fast and furious two weeks of lecturing, talking, eating, drinking and partying at Boulder, but I think everything went off well, and now I am looking forward to exploring some more of this magnificent country out here. I will try to keep Max Perkins informed of my mailing address along the way, and if anything of immediate urgency turns up I think you can always get in touch with me through him.

Good luck, and, as always, all my best and warmest wishes,
Sincerely,
Tom Wolfe

1. Although she had been dismissed as Wolfe's agent, Madeleine Boyd was claiming a commission on the sales of *Of Time and the River*. Eventually the matter was settled, and Mrs. Boyd continued to receive only her commission on sales of *Look Homeward, Angel*.

🌷 🌷 🌷 [Fall 1935]

Dear Wolfe:
Here's the carbon of the second part cut down by yrs. truly—I've already sent the original up to the Atlantic[1] but if you're going to make any corrections in this or the first part please do them PDQ because if they do decide to use it they'll want to rush it to the press since they originally had it scheduled for December. OK? I'm sorry I'd just gone out to dinner when you phoned yesterday but I guess it was about this??

Yrs   Nowell
P.S. I caught transcients for transcience in the original.

1. Nowell had already sold Wolfe's revised preface to the *Atlantic Monthly* under the title, "The Story of a Novel," when Wolfe discovered another part of it that he had used for his Colorado lecture. When the whole essay proved too long for the *Atlantic*, it was accepted by the *Saturday Review of Literature* for publication in three installments.

🌷 🌷 🌷 October 26, 1935

Dear Wolfe:
Oh God how the dollars roll in. Herewith the fourth payment on the German serial rights to "Boom Town:" $3.36 as usual.
Yours, Nowell

🌷 🌷 🌷 Nov. 1, 1935

Dear Wolfe:
I don't know whether you want or ought to come, but I want to ask you anyway. Remember I told you O'Brien (the anthologist)[1] wanted to meet you and I was going to ask him to dinner when he got back from his lecture tour? Well, I've changed it to lunch and he's coming next Thursday, the seventh. I'd rather have you than anybody if you want to come, but if it's going to keep you from working on the book or to make you unhappy, for Christ's sakes tell

me so and I'll understand. So call me up when you get this and tell me what you think and I'll plan accordingly.

Yrs, Nowell

1. Edward J. O'Brien chose "The Sun and the Rain," which had appeared in *Scribner's Magazine*, May 1934, to be included in *The Best Short Stories, 1935*.

❦ ❦ ❦   114 East 56th Street
New York
Nov. 2, 1935

Dear Wolfe:

It seems that I can't let a day go by without pestering you about something and I'm sorry but this was too good an opportunity to let slide. I guess you remember Miss Curtin,[1] the girl who used to sit up at night typing for us at Lieber's. If not, I know you've heard me talk about her lately and about what a swell girl she is. She's been running the League for Less Noise but that has just folded up on account of La Guardia's taking the whole idea over so she's started to look for another job. The minute I heard it I thought that she could be your chief cook and bottle washer and typist better than anybody even Aladine Bell, and if as you say you're going to get down to work you ought to have somebody good oughn't you? Anyway this is just a suggestion so that when you really get around to finding a typist you can get in touch with her either through me or through her husband, Jessup, in the Scribner's Bookstore, if you like the idea.

That's the chief thing on my mind and the second is about the book of short stories. I've already sent a set of galleys to Leah Salisbury[2] as I told you but I haven't got any written authorization for FROM DEATH TO MORNING since your letter only covered OF TIME AND THE RIVER. Then too I ought to start copies off to the various foreign publishers especially to Holland if we want to prevent piracy this time. I guess I already wrote you about the commissions for foreign agents. When I sent them copies of OF TIME AND THE RIVER you had gone abroad without giving me any authorization and the whole thing was such a mess that Low and I decided I'd better try to sell it without any foreign agent. That might have been possible except that the person who Low thought was your Czechoslovakian publisher turned out to be an agent instead. I therefore made a compromise with her (our old friend Vincy Schwartz) by offering her half of my 10% commission and saying that on future books I'd guarantee her the full 10%.

That's the way the matter stands now and I've just had a letter from her asking about the stories so will you maybe discuss this letter with Low and let me know what to do. The same applied to my Scandinavian agent as well because I can't help feeling that we get quicker and better results with a foreign agent than by trying to negotiate things all the way across the Atlantic. Of course, old lady Boyd charged you about 30%: 10% for her, 10% for Brandt and Brandt to whom she gave the foreign rights, and 10% to the foreign agent to whom Brandt in turn entrusted the actual sale. Not that that proves anything but then. I don't want to keep nagging at you so I shall shut up about this now that I've explained it all and if you want to write me a letter authorizing me to handle the foreign sale of the short story book that will be swell and I'll get going on it immediately.

That's all for now except for one little extra nag that I can't help:—to wit, that I'm still hoping you will get an inspiration for the Saturday Review title some time soon when you least expect it.

Yours, Nowell

P.S. Vincy says there was no option in "Look Homeward" contract and she's mailing it to you.

P.S. I just got a note from Emjo Basshe[3] saying he's got a job directing a negro theatre and guesses he'll be too busy to do "Of Time and the River" for a while—so that settles that anyway so cheer up.

1. Curtin became Wolfe's typist for several months. She also worked intermittently for Nowell.

2. A Hollywood agent who arranged for sale of literary material to the moving picture studios.

3. A New York playwright and director who had directed the production of "Roll, Sweet Chariot" by Wolfe's friend Paul Green.

Charles Scribner's Sons
597 Fifth Avenue
New York
Nov. 6, 1935

Dear Miss Nowell:

In answer to your letter of November 2nd, in which you ask me to give you written authorization to act as my agent for "From Death to Morning" in those foreign countries with which I do not already have an arrangement of my own, and also as agent with authority to deal with Miss Leah Salisbury, or any other agent concerning movie rights, I am glad to give you the authorization to act for me, and you may consider this letter as such authorization.

Sincerely yours,
Thomas Wolfe

P.S. And it is understood, of course, that the agent's commission is 10%.

                         [December 1935]
Dear Wolfe:

I was hoping you'd be here but it's just a lot of odds and ends. First, I got your O. Henry collection from Doubleday today[1] and I've borrowed it to read on the train to New Bedford—you don't mind do you? Will bring it here Monday—O.K.??

I brought the Blythe in to Mr. Perkins in case you want to look at it.[2]

Now do please be a good boy and write a lot of little "he's" in pencil over the "I's" in that piece for Caravan[3]—or have you already maybe? It's such a cinch and I'll get it retyped or whatever else you want done—

I said to Mr. Perkins if Waite was through and you wanted somebody else to dramatize the Angel or Time and the River I'd tell Salisbury and we could probably still get that girl who did Thunder or the Left and was reading the Angel when you signed with Waite. What do you think? If you could get a real businesslike professional dramatization it might mean a lot of dough?? But I'll leave it for you and MEP to discuss.

                                        Love   Nowell
Back Sunday and Curtin will run things Friday if there's any emergency.

1. "Only the Dead Know Brooklyn" appeared in *O. Henry Memorial Award: Prize Stories of 1935.*

2. Since LeGette Blythe was the literary editor of the *Charlotte Observer*, this was probably some brief notice of Wolfe's work.

3. An excerpt from Wolfe's proposed book, *The Hills beyond Pentland*, which was later revised into the material about the Joyners and included in Chapter 2 of *The Web and the Rock.*

                 114 East 56th Street
                                       New York
                                       Dec 27, 1935
Dear Wolfe:

Here is the piece from the Pentland book which I just phoned you about, and which is due at Caravan before January if you think it's OK to send. The only things I did to it were to take out the incident about Bob Patton and his top hat which was in "Web of Earth," and to change a few "I's" to "He's" or "Eugene's." Maybe that sounds wrong in some places because the story within a story made it harder than usual to get clear, but you'll see anyway.

Oh yes, and is "wing" on page 11 right, or should it be "wink." Maybe "wing" is a colloquialism that I just don't know.

I really think that's all and I hope you'll think it's all right because it really is a swell piece. I'm mailing a copy to Perkins too, so he can see what I'm up to.

Yrs   Nowell

P.S. And I did have such a swell time Xmas.

🌱   🌱   🌱
New Bedford
Saturday, Jan. 4 [1936]

Dear Wolfe:

There are some odds and ends of business that I'm always wanting to ask you but I never get around to because I hate to bother you when you're upset about going to Washington or working against the Saturday Review deadline or something like that. So rather than take a chance of phoning next week and either waking you up or interrupting your work I may as well write them now so that you needn't bother with them until you feel like it.

The first is, you don't mind if I switch from Salisbury to somebody else do you? She's now started a regular book and magazine department which puts her too much in the same field as me to be a good agent for my movie rights, and I'm more than justified in leaving her because she's been neglecting my people more or less lately in favor of her own. She was all right about your books but I can never get her to pay decent attention to the good but less famous people like Alvah Bessie[1] etc. etc., or even to be there when I phone her about them, so I'm taking them away and I think it would be far better to take you too. I've got a new agent in Hollywood working on Bessie (J. M. Lansinger who has just started lately and represents Lieber there, Herz, and various other agents, and who seems to be turning out damn well. He used to own College Humor and his associate is one Dorothy Ann Blank, who was editor of that sheet but with really decent taste in spite of it. I know enough from her reactions to Bessie to know she'd be terribly excited about representing somebody really fine like you and it might mean that we could stir up some new excitement there on the coast about either Of Time and the River or the stories.) So I'd like to get your and Perkins' reactions to this so that I could switch as soon as I get everything ready to break the news to Salisbury and really authorize Lansinger. ????

The other thing is intensely personal and the sort of thing that I hate to talk about for fear of seeming like Lieber, even though I really do think it's fair in this case. That is, do you think I'm due a commission on the book sales of The Story of a Novel? Of course I've never taken one and never will on the regular novels because I haven't anything to do with those, and I realize that the few stories that I gouged out while you were away were a minor part of "Death to Morning" as compared to the really big things like "Web of Earth" and "Death the Proud Brother." But I did work terribly hard on The Story of a Novel and [had] the faith to do it way back last summer when nobody else was paying much attention to it and it might easily have got lost or never polished and cut or still lying around somewhere at Scribner's or your house.

Well, I've been stewing over this backwards and forwards for weeks now and I still hate to say it because as you so succinctly put it that day at the Park Lane you did make me when I left Lieber last year, far more than Nancy² or Joffe, and the one thing I don't want ever to be is ungrateful or mercenary in return. It's chiefly because I spend more time on things than I can afford because I have to pay Curtin to help me keep things up to date and that means that I'm losing money lately rather than making it and it seems more sensible to admit it now than to go on being proud or shy. Oh jesus, this sounds now as if I was trying to make you pity me which I didn't mean, but just to explain more or less. The more I say the worse I make it sound so I guess I'll stop right here and leave it entirely to you and what you think is right. [several words crossed out]

So don't hurry about it but think it over to talk it over with Perkins or whatever you want, and however you decide is all right with me. That crossed out place is where I stopped and smoked a cigarette and almost threw the whole damn letter away because it does sound pretty damn mean and grasping and as if I ought to be ashamed and proud to work for you for nothing if it ever was necessary, and I really think I would be, believe it or not. But I guess I ought to be brazen this time and go ahead and mail this so that at least I'll stop worrying about it pro and con and you can decide it however you want to once and for all.

Yrs very embarrassed
Nowell

1. A novelist and later soldier in the Lincoln Brigade during the Spanish Civil War with whom Nowell worked during the period she was associated with the Maxim Lieber agency.

2. Nancy Hale, granddaughter of Edward Everett Hale and author of such novels as

The Young Die Good and *A New England Girlhood*, was represented by Nowell's agency.

                    114 East 56th Street
                                       New York
                                       February 4, 1936

Dear Wolfe:

Here at last is the money from the Saturday Review for "The Story of a Novel." It's the first decent-sized check since November, so I've deducted the odds and ends of typing I had done for you etc. etc. as follows:

typing Bacchus Pentland piece for Caravan	$3.45
Extra copies Sat Rev for abroad	1.20
12 copies Sunday Times for Review of Death to Morning for abroad	1.20
Daily news papers for ditto	1.08
Total	6.93
plus my 10% commission	15.00
	21.93

Which, deducted from $150 makes $128.07

This covers all the little expenses to date, and begins from where I itemized them for you in my letter of October 24 and received a check therefor from you through Scribner's. It all sounds complicated as hell but the point is that everything is square now.

Hope everything is going along fine.

Yrs   Nowell

                    March 11, 1936

Dear Wolfe:

Herewith another little dribble from Germany which represents the fifth payment on the German serial rights on BOOM TOWN.

I have been dickering with your friend, Mr. Erich A. Walter, and have raised his $10 bid to $25 on reprinting HIS FATHER'S EARTH,[1] so that's another little dribble to look forward to in the distant future,—when the ESSAY ANNUAL is finally published.

Yours, Nowell

1. Published in *Modern Monthly*, April 1935, and later became a part of Chapter 2 in *The Web and the Rock*. Erich Walter selected it for reprinting in the 1936 *Essay Annual*.

114 East 56th Street
New York
March 17, 1936

Dear Wolfe:

I'm sending this to Scribner's instead of 1st Avenue because otherwise I'm afraid you'll forget and never mail it back. But I'm enclosing a stamped envelope so if you just sign your name on the enclosed hunk of paper and give the whole works to Miss Wyckoff[1] then she'll stick it in the office mail for you. The point is that Scott Foresman who are the publishers of the Eric A. Walter "Essay Annual" want to have the autographs of the contributors on the jacket of said annual and want you to write yours for them. So as long as I got them up from $10 to $25 on "His Father's Earth" I guess we can throw in an autograph too for that purpose.

My eyes are lousy to-night so I won't write any more. I haven't had a chance at the Fisher[2] yet so maybe you'd better glance through a copy at the store, though I will eventually when I catch up with myself and get rid of this headache.

Hope everything is O.K. and the Jersey expeditionary force was a complete victory.

Yours, Nowell

1. Irma Wyckoff was Maxwell Perkins's secretary.
2. Vardis Fisher's novel, *No Villain Need Be*, a volume of his autobiographical tetralogy that contained some material about his years in New York when he first knew Wolfe at New York University.

114 East 56th Street
New York
April 21, 1936

P.S. This is the next noon and I've reread it in hopes that it would look better in the daylight. I know its a mess and I am too but at least its sincere and I may as well get it off my chest and mail it in hopes you'll understand.

Dear Wolfe:

I guess you didn't really mean what you said on the phone but it's two thirty and I can't go to sleep again until I get it off my chest, so here goes and I hope you don't mind. Because I can't help being terribly hurt if you really think I'm a leech sucking unearned commissions out of you, and I can't help objecting because I honestly don't think you realize how much time and effort it takes to do a job like "The Story of a Novel." Sure, you did speak to Canby[1] about it yourself, but before that I'd done a helluva lot of work and so please let me retrace the whole history of it in self-justification.

Way back in March 35 when I was helping you get out of Brooklyn and was sorting the manuscript, you gave me part of the preface and said that there might be something in it and would I get the "artist in America" part back from Sanderson Vanderbilt. So after a letter and several phone calls I got it from him and kept it until you came back from Germany when I gave it to you, and you and Mr. Perkins left it in some bar somewhere. So then when you were going to Colorado you gave me the first half of the second, dictated version and said for me to see what I could do. Well, I knew the chances were only about four for a thing like that but anyway I thought it was so terribly fine that I took it to the hospital with me and cut it from about 15000 to 7000. (I'm not sure of the exact figures now but if you look at the manuscript I worked on which I later gave to Perkins you can see all the laborious little brackets.)

I know you think cutting like that is easy, but it really is the hardest thing in the world and the one which takes most patience, going over and over and taking out just a few words at a time and putting back half of them in an effort to be sure not to slaughter your meaning, and then counting up the whole estimate and finding it STILL much too long and reading the whole thing over in a search for more words to come out and then estimating etc. etc. and with it always too long until at the end of a good week's work you're sure that it's as tight as it can be without butchering. Oh Jesus, I'm not complaining because it's worth it in your case, but what I'm trying to say is that I spent tremendous effort on it and I can get corroboration from my two trained nurses, Mother (who added up the words taken out as I called them to her), the typist who finally copied that first draft, and finally Mother and a friend who read back the typist's copy to be sure she'd got all the little brackets and brackets within brackets right.

Well, I can see you sneering, but it's not the least exaggerated and you can ask Perkins for the copy if you don't believe me. So then I sent the article to the Yale Review, they declined it, and I sold it to the Atlantic. Whereupon you told me there'd been a mistake and the second half was missing and brought it around to me and I cut that in a rush job from around 15000 to 7000, couldn't sell it to the Atlantic too, recalled it at your request and sent it to Canby after those two or three evening sessions with you, or rather one with you and two or three more waiting for you with you unhappy about coming and getting here late and making me feel like a goddamned old-maid school-teacher and bawling like a baby when you started to open my beer with my kid glove. Oh Lord, I didn't mean to bring that up and I know it's my own fault for taking things so seriously, but I just can't help it and it always makes me so wretched the way I am now.

I'm not complaining because you know damn well that the thrill of working on your stuff is worth it in the long run, but it does hurt my feelings terribly to be told that I'm no damn good and a parasite on you and a money-grubbing jew because I think I deserve a commission on the thing all the way through instead of $15 on the Saturday Review sale when that barely covers my expense of hiring Curtin to relieve me from my regular work to do that last rush job of cutting the second half. Besides I really and honestly think that the book would have remained one of those things you were going to do some day, or that Perkins didn't have time to work in, unless I'd salvaged it and cut it and sold it and it had got such swell critical recognition. But it isn't any of that that matters so much as feeling that somebody hates you when you've done your goddamndest working for them and when the whole thing seems unjust and bitter.

Well, this is just plain hysterical now and I know you hate hysterical women more than anything on earth and I apologize, but when I'm so terribly unhappy about a thing the only way is to pour it out and get it over instead of letting it eat me and make me act like a goddamned crybaby sometime if I ran into you at Scribner's. I don't care so much about the money even though I do think it's only fair and if you still think I'm a blood-sucker after reading this attempt at justification, all right, I won't take the money. I got copies from Scribner's for foreign countries except Germany and England because Perkins thought it was all right for me not to bother you about it as long as I was the agent for the thing but maybe that was wrong too though I wasn't grabbing but just trying to leave you in the peace you need to do good work. Well, I don't know if any of this makes any sense or not but I hope you'll understand somehow and let me know something and not keep me hanging in mid air this way. I spose I'm a sap to let myself get in such a state over anybody or anything, but I just can't help it so please forgive me and I guess this is all for tonight.

Yrs   Nowell

1. Henry Seidel Canby, the editor of the *Saturday Review of Literature*.

114 East 56th Street
New York
May 12, 1936

Dear Wolfe:

I forgot to give you the Blythe column[1] last night what with all the excitement and everything so here it is and I think you'll like it.

And I guess it goes without saying that I had a swell time last night. All kidding aside you're a damn fine host and it did my old heart good to see you beaming at everybody and really liking them. After all that's what makes the world go round and there is nothing like it and I keep thinking of it today. Or am I getting just plain senti-mental-sententious? Anyway, more power to you and thanks loads and here's hoping for lots of dough so you can give parties whenever you want. The money for the English Harper's Bazaar use of "In the Park" is due to come through from the English bank pretty soon now, only fifty or sixty bucks but it's something to look forward to and I'll be shooting it over as soon as it clears through the exchange.

Yrs. Nowell

1. An item about Wolfe from the *Charlotte Observer*.

114 East 56th Street
New York
May 22, 1936

Dear Wolfe:

Just a line to report progress. I gave Mr. Perkins the other copy of Mrs. Saunders'[1] piece about you and he says he thinks it's all right. So I'll write her that you both think so and then we can forget it.

I got Palmer on the phone and it looks as if he was going to take the story and you needn't do anything about it. What he's planning to have is a late-summer number, probably August, with specimens of work in progress by you, Dos Passos, Faulkner, and maybe Fisher. He says he isn't absolutely positive yet until he sees if he can get the others lined up all right, but will let us know later. He also says that the Mercury is going to publish articles against the New Deal and that for that reason Farley[2] is apt to watch like a hawk for anything censorable. Just to be on the safe side he thinks he'll want to cut out a few phrases here and there, but he's going to draw little pencil marks on the ones he's worried about and will send it to me so you can approve it. In other words, everything is O.K. and you can just forget it till he does that. He said he was planning to pay around $200, was that what they told you? If they told you more let me know, but I think that was it and it's about tops for them as far as I've heard to date.

Guess this is all for now except I hope you're getting along swell and I catch myself grinning in a gratified sort of way every time I think of Scribner's being handed down to fame with all its unsung heroes, not to mention villains.[3]

Yrs hastily
Nowell

1. Sally Saunders, editor of the *Junior League Magazine*, who had interviewed Wolfe's mother when she was visiting Asheville and who had written an essay about Wolfe and the "Old Kentucky Home" boarding house.

2. James Farley, postmaster general during the Roosevelt administration.

3. This has reference to the fact that Wolfe had begun writing about the literary world, basing several of his characters on prominent members of his publishing house, Charles Scribner's Sons.

During the spring of 1936, Wolfe made a decision that eventually changed the course of his career. In answer to criticism in the literary press that he was confined to the path of autobiographical fiction, he decided to write a novel that would not be part of the planned Eugene Gant series. This work, entitled "The Vision of Spangler's Paul," was to be about a young man who finds that everything in life turns out to be different from what he expected. But since all the fiction that Wolfe produced had its source in his personal experience, this new book gradually began to absorb everything that he had written or planned for the Eugene Gant cycle, until as months went by it developed into a new autobiographical chronicle.

After work on the new project was well advanced, Wolfe took a vacation trip to Berlin to see the Olympic Games, an experience that led him to perceive that Germany under Nazi domination was something different from what he had thought while blinded by fame the previous year. This led to his creation of a short novel, "I Have a Thing to Tell You," in which his hero witnessed the arrest of a Jew who was attempting to escape from Germany while traveling as a train passenger.

Meanwhile, Miss Nowell continued to find markets easily for Wolfe's fictional episodes, almost all of which she had to shorten in order to meet the space requirements of magazine editors.

❧ ❧ ❧

114 East 56th Street
New York
June 15. 1936

Dear Wolfe:

Just to report the state of the nation. Palmer says up till Friday will be all right for the title. Palmer phoned me and asked me what he should say about which book this was and what title. I'd already asked Perkins if he was willing to have Palmer announce the big news[1] and he'd said he thought it was much better not to but to wait until later. So after consulting Perkins again on the phone I told Palmer that the title of this book was as yet undecided, that it would be published next, however, instead of "October Fair"'s being published next as was announced. I left it unsaid whether this was in the Time and The River series or not. So this is just to tip you off in case he meets you anywhere or anybody asks you. O.K.?

Yours, Nowell

1. Wolfe had begun a new novel, "The Vision of Spangler's Paul," which was not a volume in the series about Eugene Gant.

114 East 56th Street
New York
June 19, 1936

Dear Wolfe:

Here's the check from Mercury for "My Father's Courthouse" (?)[1] or what-have-you.

Yours   Nowell

1. "The Bell Remembered," *American Mercury*, August 1936, was the first published section of Wolfe's new project. It later appeared as Chapters 9 and 10 of *The Hills Beyond*.

114 East 56th Street
New York
July 10, 1936

Dear Wolfe:

Here is a copy of the letter I've just received from Leah Salisbury releasing your movie rights completely. I'm sending copies to Mitchell and Perkins too so that there will be plenty of them if we ever have to look for them. And of course I'll keep the original in my files.

Your cleaning lady, Mrs. Mitchell, called me up because she knew you'd gone away without a suitcase and kept worrying about you. She seemed terribly nice so I phoned Perkins to check up on you and then reassured Mrs. M that everything was OK. I just thought you'd be touched by her solicitude and like to know she was so fine about it.

Hope you've had a swell vacation and not married any lady landowners. Am looking forward to reading George Hauser[1] when you get back and have time.

Yours, Nowell

1. "No More Rivers," the first item that Wolfe wrote about the publishers, "The House of Rodney." The character, George Hauser, was based on Wallace Meyer, an editor at Scribner's. For Wolfe's final version of this story, see "No More Rivers" in this volume.

114 East 56th Street
                                                       New York
                                                       July 23, 1936

Dear Wolfe:

No this is not Christmas, but just the Vardis Fisher books which I
promised to mail so that you would be spared carrying them all the
way to Germany.[1] The tetralogy you already know about, so I won't
say anything about it except that foreign rights were supposed to
have been handled by Curtis Brown for Doubleday on these books.
For that reason, in case Rowohlt likes them, they would probably
have to make the contract with Frau Wegner, who is the German
representative of Curtis Brown. However, if they want to let me
know about it instead so that I can tell Fisher and Doubleday, it
will be all right of course, although my position in this case will
be unofficial.

I don't know, but it might be that Rowohlt might consider some of
the statements in the last book a little bit too radical, even though
Fisher certainly is far from that himself. Perhaps those could be
deleted without any trouble. However, in case they are adamant
about the tetralogy I'm also sending you my own personal copy of
DARK BRIDEWELL, which I think is really superb and probably
easier to publish (being only one book, etc., etc.) than the tetralogy. I
guess you read BRIDEWELL in the old days at N.Y.U., but if you
didn't be sure to skim through it because I know it's something
you'll be completely nuts over. The agent to handle the foreign rights
on that book, the Lord and Fisher only know, but I could easily
arrange it with him in any case.

As for his future work, the situation is as follows: his novelette,
APRIL, is the book that I'm now negotiating on that triple contract
between Doubleday and Caxton. Whether I will handle the foreign
rights, or whether they will go to Doubleday is undecided. But everything will be more definite by the time these books reach you. It is
not as big and important a book as the tetralogy but it might be
easier for Rowohlt to begin with it, by that same token. I wish I had
some copy of it I could send you, but I guess we'll just have to wait
until galley-proofs are available—or some such. Fisher is going to
start work in a week or so on another book, and a very important
one, which he thinks is going to be his masterpiece and will bring
him way up to the top. You know how writers hate to talk about
their books before they get going on them so you won't be surprised
to hear that he's been pretty mysterious about it so far. Whether it's
going to be a historical novel on the Mormons or not, I don't know;

I know that's one of the very swell ideas he has in his mind so the chances are that he may carry it out. At any rate I will write him and ask him if he will talk a little about his plans so that I can pass the word on to you and Frere-Reeves and Rowohlt, etc., etc. I'll get another letter off to you as soon as I hear from him, but in the meanwhile I want to start these books off because parcel-post is pretty damn slow.

I do hope you're having the swellest time in the whole world, and a good rest to boot.

Yours, Nowell

1. On his trip to Germany to see the Olympic Games, Wolfe intended to try to interest Rowohlt Verlag in publishing German translations of Vardis Fisher's novels.

Postcard
Berlin–Charlottenburg
View of Budapesterstrasse,
   Eingang Zool. Garten
Aug. 7, 1936

Dear Nowell:

I've shown Rowohlt and Ledig[1] all your letters and pumped up Fisher until they're all excited—but where the hell are the books?— They haven't come yet. Having a good time—saw all my friends— met lots of new people—interviews, drawings in paper, Olympic Games, etc.—this town beautifully clean and cool after N.Y.
P.S. Monday Aug. 10—Books came today!

1. Heinz Ledig, the illegitimate son of Ernst Rowolht, had become Wolfe's closest friend in Germany. The character, Franz Heildig, in "I Have a Thing to Tell You" (and also in *You Can't Go Home Again*) is based on Ledig.

114 East 56th Street
New York
August 21, 1936

Dear Wolfe:

Here is the money from the sale of FAME AND THE POET[1] to the Mercury. The check was $260 and I have deducted my commission as well as $6.75 which was the typing charge on NO MORE RIVERS.

Yours, Nowell

1. Published in the *American Mercury*, October 1936.

Postcard
                                            View of Rattenberg
                                            Aug. 27 1936
On my way back to Munich and Berlin and if I can get passage—all
boats crowded—I'll see you in a week or so—
                                            Love—Wolfe—

                        114 East 56th Street
                                            New York
                                            August 27, 1936
Dear Wolfe:
    I think this story has gone through so many changes that it would
be better for me to show it to you rather than go ahead with Cosmopolitan or somewhere and then have you dissatisfied with it when it
comes out in print. I already wrote you about how strongly Perkins
and Meyer felt about it so while I was home for the weekend I took
out that whole piece that they objected to and skipped right over to
where he gets up out of bed.[1] I sent it back to Perkins and am enclosing his letter so that you can see what he says. Frankly, I don't
know—I am still completely sold on all the descriptions of the river
and the city as well as on the very swell telephone call. I do guess that
my having to take so much out has made it a little thinner than it was
in the beginning, but I honestly worked so long on the piece and got
so fond of it that I can't form a disinterested opinion any more. I
called up Perkins and said I guessed I'd better show it to you especially since he was so lukewarm about it in its present form. Well, I
do hope that all this won't spoil your holiday, but it seemed the only
sensible thing to do under the circumstances. If Waxman[2] begins to
ask about it I'll simply tell him that it has to wait for your return so
that you can approve the cuts. So there really won't be any loss by
delaying a little while, and I won't be going ahead and exceeding
my authority.
    Hope you're having a swell time. Mrs. Mitchell called up and
said she had a card from you and that everything was all right, so I
told her just to keep an eye on the apartment and that you would
probably be back sometime in September. Don't worry about anything because all is under control.
                                            Yours, Nowell

    1. Perkins and Meyer had objected to a section of "No More Rivers," which satir-
ized Charles Scribner and other members of the firm.
    2. Percy Waxman, associate editor of *Cosmopolitan* magazine.

🌷 🌷 🌷   Postcard
                                          Munich—View of the Feldherrn-
                                              halle
                                          (Taubenfütterung)
                                          [postmark September 8, 1936]

This is a wonderful city—after eight years it seems very natural and
friendly—Frankly, after what happened last year, I don't very much
want to come "home"—but I will.

🌷 🌷 🌷   Postcard
                                          View of Paris—La Place de
                                              L'Opera
                                          [postmark September 14, 1936]

Dear Miss Nowell:
    Don't do anything about the stories until I get back—I've written
a good piece over here—I'm afraid it may mean that I can't come
back to the place where I am liked best and have the most friends—
but I've decided to publish it. So wait on me—Wolfe—

🌷 🌷 🌷   Postcard
                                          View of Paris—La Madeleine
                                          [undated, mid-September, 1936,
                                              and unmailed]

Dear Nowell:
    I've written a wonderful piece—after it gets published I won't be
able to go back to the place where I'm liked best and have more
friends than anywhere else in the world—but I'm going to publish it
(or what's a heaven for?)—I'm going to call it (for various reasons)
"I Have A Thing To Tell You"—which may not be so foolish as
it sounds.   W.

🌷 🌷 🌷   114 East 56th Street
                                          New York
                                          October 5, 1936

Dear Wolfe:
    The North German Lloyd girl[1] called me up today and asked if
you were back, saying she wanted one of those articles from you
soon. I decided it was better for me not to go putting my foot in it
but to let you write her whatever you thought best. So I just said
you'd only been back a few days and that I'd tell you she called.

Hope that was O.K. and you can cope with her all right.

> Yours in haste
> Nowell

P.S. Isn't your phone in—I thought you said it was. I tried to phone you about this, but they insisted it was still disconnected. Or are they just dumb?

1. Wolfe had made an agreement with North German Lloyd to write three articles for their trade magazine, *Seven Seas*, in return for a half-price passage on one of their ocean liners sailing to Germany.

                    865 First Avenue
                                        New York, N.Y.
                                        Oct. 5 1936

Dear Miss Nowell:

By this time the contents of that birthday bottle of champagne has gone where so many of the good things of life go; but the memory of it,—and more than *it*—of the generous spirit of its giver will never go. Thank you for giving my birthday a touch of gaiety and joy it should otherwise have sadly wanted. A thousand thanks!

> Yours gratefully,
> Wolfe

                    [postmark
                                        Oct. 6, 1936]

Dear Wolfe:

Bless your heart, you didn't have to go to all that work of writing me, and so terribly legibly at that. I am very much touched and shall treasure same, and hereby guarantee that it will never appear in the market place of Mr. Reuter (sp?) Dooher,[1] or anybody. Love

> Nowell

1. Wolfe had given some of his manuscripts to Murdach Dooher, a young friend who was beginning a dealership in rare books and manuscripts, to sell them on commission to libraries and collectors. When Dooher sold manuscripts and kept the money himself, Wolfe had to undertake a lawsuit to get his manuscripts back. Barnet Ruder, a rare book dealer, was a witness to testify for Wolfe when the case came before the court.

❦   ❦   ❦
114 East 56th Street
New York
October 28, 1936

Dear Wolfe:

Know ye by this token that Miss Martha Dodd[1] is landing in New York on the Manhattan this Friday. Henrietta Hertz called me up and asked me to tell you because she was shy about bothering you herself. She says Martha is staying in an apartment with no phone so there really doesn't seem to be much way that you can get in touch with her, except through Henrietta—if you want to. So I'll leave it up to you to do whatever you want about it.

Hope you are getting along o.k. with everything. Let me know if you you want anything.

Yours, in haste,
Nowell

1. The daughter of Ambassador William E. Dodd, whom Wolfe had met at the Embassy in Berlin in the summer of 1935. She and Wolfe had a brief and rather wild love affair.

❦   ❦   ❦
114 East 56th Street
New York
November 3, 1936

Dear Wolfe:

The chances are that Scribner's sent you one of the statements on "The Story of a Novel" along with your other ones for Time and the River and so forth, but they sent me one too so I want to be sure you get it. I've checked the figures and see they did give you 15% after all which is fine, and I've kept a copy of it here for the file. You'll see the money isn't actually due until February 21,[1] so when the time comes we can decide whether Scribner's is to send me the check, or the check for ten percent, or you the check and let you give me whatever you think fair, or none at all because even though you said you were going to give it to me I'd rather not take it than have you feel it wasn't fair. So anyway, we don't have to worry about it for months and months yet, and I'll leave it entirely up to you.

I got a letter from my Scandinavian agent saying that Steenske of Oslo hasn't been able to get the Norwegian edition of "Of Time and the River" out this fall after all because Hans Heiberg, the good translator who did "Look Homeward, Angel" and is to do "Of Time and the River," got an "eye-decease" and had to lay off work for a while. They think the book will sell better if published in a fall season than a spring one, which is sposed to be comparatively piddling in

Scandinavia, so they want to put it off till next fall. I've written them that I think it's better to stick to Heiberg rather than to get some inferior man and a man with a different style from "Look Homeward, Angel" but the time extension only runs till January 1938 so they can't stall forever and you needn't worry.

And now about something else which isn't the least important and which I hate to bother you about. Maybe you remember a long letter I showed you once from a very young and very good writer in Louisiana who was a specially ardent Wolfe fan. His name was Charles Martin and I've sold his novel about the Cajuns to Soskin,[2] as I guess I must have told you now and then, having him very much and very happily on my mind. Because he was influenced by you so much (but not in an imitative way) Soskin is sending you a complimentary copy, and if you should possibly like it and want to say so, Martin and Soskin would be in the seventh heaven. I guess I would too, but it's dead against all of my principals [sic] to bother you about this sort of thing, both for the sake of your book and because it always makes me sore as hell when people try to get favors out of your warm-hearted self. This time I was torn between two of my children, because Martin really is fine and knowing how he admired you I didn't have the heart to refuse. But if you don't want to bother just pay no attention to it and I'll explain about you being busy working, etc. etc.

Well, I guess this is the end of a very long and incoherent letter, but I'm rushing through it to go out and do my duty by Roosevelt before my Liberty League mother hits town.

Yours, Nowell

P.S. One more thing. I saw Logan[3] and he is very anxious to get a story or more from you. I told him you were working on the book, but he wanted me to be sure to convey the message to you as against the time when you did start selling the new stories.

1. Scribner's had asked Wolfe to accept a royalty of 10 percent because they expected a limited sale and because they planned to set a price of only one dollar for this rather slim book. But when the book came out at a price of $1.50 and was widely reviewed and well received, Wolfe complained that he should receive his usual 15 percent royalty.

2. William Soskin was the executive editor of Howell Soskin Publishers. He had once been on a panel of judges that had awarded Wolfe a prize of $2,500 for "A Portrait of Bascom Hawke" in the Scribner Short Novel Contest.

3. Harlan Logan, editor-publisher of *Scribner's Magazine*. Dashiell had been fired in a reorganization of the editorial staff.

❦ ❦ ❦

114 East 56th Street
New York
November 17, 1936

Dear Wolfe:

Crichton[1] wants to know if you'd want to come to a party at his house in Bronxville Sunday at 4:30 or so for the George Seldeses.[2] I told him you were working etc. but he was so full of enthusiasm and everything that I said I'd ask you anyway. So maybe if it isn't too much work would you give me a ring so he won't think I'm being snooty.

The other thing you may know, which is that you're in Who's Who this year. Jessup in the bookstore called me up to tell me, so if you want to know what they say I'll get him to copy it out and mail it to you. Or did you get one or don't you care? It's just the usual thing about where born, what written etc., of course, but J. says they mention Bascom Hawke and The Web of Earth as well as the novels & other books.

No more now, and I hope this won't interrupt the big job.

Yours, Nowell

1. Kyle Crichton was an associate editor of *Scribner's Magazine* who was interested in left-wing causes and who sometimes wrote for *New Masses* under the name Robert Forsythe.

2. George Seldes, a left-wing journalist, best known perhaps for his book, *The Lords of the Press*, 1936.

PART V ❧ January to September 1937
Wolfe Revisits the South

During 1937 Wolfe traveled to the South three times. First he went
to New Orleans, and on his return to New York he stopped off at
Chapel Hill, North Carolina, where he renewed acquaintance with
friends he had known in his college days at the university. He had not
returned to his hometown of Asheville, North Carolina, since 1929,
because the publication of Look Homeward, Angel had caused
scandal and had angered many of his fellow townspeople who found
themselves and their friends portrayed satirically in the novel. But
Wolfe met with such a friendly reception in Chapel Hill that he
decided in late spring to travel home to Asheville. Because the
passage of time and the development of Wolfe's literary fame had
softened opinion in the town, he was received with warmth and
acclaim—so much so that he decided to return in July to spend the
summer months in the Asheville vicinity.

But in his return to the South, Wolfe was also acting upon a desire
to retreat from the New York literary scene. The previous year he
had been the target of an ill-natured attack by Bernard De Voto,
who, in an article "Genius Is Not Enough" in the Saturday Review
of Literature, had declared that Wolfe was unable to function without Perkins. Recently Wolfe had quarreled with Perkins himself
because Perkins had objected to Wolfe's satirical sketches (as yet
unpublished) of members of the Scribner staff. Most serious of all,
Wolfe had become involved in three lawsuits, one of which, a libel
action brought by a woman whom he had portrayed as "Mad
Maude" in From Death to Morning, had wiped out all his earnings
and had left him indebted to Scribner's for over $1,100. When
Perkins and other officials at Scribner's had not wanted to take on
the legal expenses of a defense and had persuaded him to settle out of
court, Wolfe had felt betrayed, and after brooding over the decision
all summer, he began to seek another publisher.

During this time, Elizabeth Nowell continued to sell a sufficient
number of stories so that Wolfe had enough money to live on from
month to month. The most important were "The Child by Tiger," the
story of a Negro who went on a rampage of random shooting in a
Southern town and was lynched by raging vigilante pursuers, and
"The Lost Boy," Wolfe's recapture of the memory of his brother
Grover who had died when Tom himself was only three years old.

❦ ❦ ❦   Jan 13 1937
ELIZABETH NOWELL 114 EAST FIFTY SIXTH STREET
HAVE REVISED ADDITION THINK IMPROVED GERMAN
PIECE[1] HAVE CUT TO ABOUT FIFTEEN THOUSAND FIND
OUT IF POSSIBLE THE EARLIEST DATE NEW REPUBLIC WILL
PUBLISH AND THE GREATEST LENGTH POSSIBLE FOR PUB-
LICATION WIRE ANSWER IMMEDIATELY BUENAVISTA
HOTEL BILOXI MISSISSIPPI.

                          TOM WOLFE

     1. "I Have a Thing to Tell You," which was scheduled to appear in the *New Republic*, March 10, 17, and 24, 1937. Wolfe was making an extended trip through the South at this time.

❦ ❦ ❦   Jan 18, 1937
Thomas Wolfe
Care Frank Graham Pres UNC
NEW REPUBLIC FRANTIC THREATENING TO DECLINE
STORY IF CANNOT USE FEBRUARY CAN YOU MAIL ME
COPY NOW IF YOU SEE PROOF LATER

                  NOWELL

❦ ❦ ❦   114 East 56th Street
                     New York
                     January 19, 1937

Dear Wolfe:
     This is to greet you as soon as you get home so that we will be sure not to lose any time about the New Republic story. They have been calling me up ever since I got your telegram to ask if the manuscript has appeared yet and they are threatening to postpone or maybe even not be able to use it if we can't get it to them by February 1st. It seems that they want to use it as the "spearhead" of the spring fiction promotion and are in a terrible state wondering whether to write it up in their announcements or not.

     So give me a ring when you get here and I think everything will be o.k.

                   Yours   Nowell

[Chapel Hill, North Carolina]
                                              Sunday, Jan. 24, 1937

Dear Nowell:

I have been unable to do much to this first instalment since coming here[1]—people have swarmed around me—old friends I have not seen in seventeen years or so—and there has been no time for anything—I went over the first half of this instalment and made—or rather indicated—a few cuts. If you and the New Republic think them good, make them: if not, you can leave it as it stands. This first section is something over 5000 words but I have found it very hard to cut. I intend to be back in New York Wednesday and will call you then.

                                              Yours, Wolfe

                                          Sunday Jan 24, 1937

—I wish you could wait with this till Wednesday. Wouldn't the N.R. let you? I'm worried about a lot of things—phonetics, accents, etc. I'm not yet sure what to do about all the "zis," "zat," "zese," "zen" business. I want to use as little as possible and yet to be consistent. I must either do without them entirely—or use them constantly. Please go through the mss. and, if you think best, make it consistent—that is get all the "th" sounds consistent—'fazzer,' 'mozzer,' 'zis,' 'zat' etc.—The character I had in mind[2] really did not speak such a marked or broken accent—yet he *did* have an accent, and I had to suggest it somehow. Have I overdone it? Wait till Wednesday if you can.

                                                  T.W.

1. Wolfe was visiting Chapel Hill, North Carolina, but was still apprehensive about a return to his hometown, Asheville, where *Look Homeward, Angel* had provoked much hostility because of the easily recognized portraits of many of its citizens.
2. Franz Heildig modeled after Heinz Ledig.

                                          114 East 56th Street
                                          New York
                                          March 4, 1937

Dear Wolfe:

I've been cutting like mad ever since it came and have got it down to ten thousand and a half by dint of cutting *very* stringently.[1] The chances are you'll object to some of the cuts, but anyway look it over, and maybe you'll want Miss H. to type it after you've got through. I guess Cosmo would really insist on 10,000 at the most but if it spoils it then we can always try Redbook, or maybe Saturday

Evening Post, telling them if they want to use it in 2 installments, you'll make more of a break around p. 28. It sure is swell although surely not usual popular magazine stuff, but you never can tell when stories are as fine as this.

Yours, Nowell

P.S. Do you think Miss H. could get a nice typewriter ribbon—the other was so faint I used the carbon and I think it might strain editors' eyes and make them like it less than otherwise.

   1. Probably "The Child by Tiger," which was published in the *Saturday Evening Post*, September 11, 1937, and later appeared as Chapter 8 in *The Web and the Rock*.

❧ ❧ ❧   March 5, 1937

Dear Wolfe:

   I guess this will help keep you out of mischief all right Saturday afternoon. I've cut hell out of it[1] but finally got it down to within 100 words of the forty pages Balmer[2] said it would have to be. A lot of the places will probably make your heart bleed because I wouldn't have thought of cutting them except in desperation. But anyway, look them over and see where they need smoothing out and maybe rewriting a little, and what you think about the whole business. And if any of them seem too outrageous to you maybe you can find some other way.

Yours, Nowell

   1. "The Lost Boy," published in *Redbook*, November 1937.
   2. Edwin Balmer, editor of *Redbook* magazine.

❧ ❧ ❧   114 East 56th Street
                                    New York
                                    March 15, 1937

Dear Wolfe:

   Miss Wyckoff says they haven't paid you for STORY OF A NOVEL yet but I think it will be coming along to me pretty soon.

   And here is the first installment from the New Republic which came to $95, minus my $9.50 leaves $85.50. The Irish piece[1] is in the mail on the way back to me and I'm going to start on it the minute I get it.

   So no more now but I'll be shooting it over very soon.

Yours, Nowell

   1. "Mr. Malone," a satirical sketch of a literary critic based on Ernest Boyd, Madeleine Boyd's husband, which was published in the *New Yorker*, May 29, 1937.

❦ ❦ ❦ 114 East 56th Street
New York
March 16, 1937

Dear Wolfe:

Here's the Malone piece all cut to hell for you to look over and do whatever you want to. I was sposed to get it down around 3000 words, but I was also sposed to "be sure not to leave anything important out" (to quote Mrs. White),[1] so around 4000 is the best I can possibly do, and at that it jerks a little in spots, I'm afraid. Well, anyway, see what you think it needs and I think probably the New Yorker will make an exception for you, even though only 2500 is their usual length.

I'm also enclosing the carbon of The Lost Boy for you to look over those few phrases that bother you. I have another copy here, so you can tell me the things you want left out on the phone I guess. Though if it's going to be very complicated you'd better send this copy back when you're ready for a messenger so I can pass it on to Balmer and Miss Miller.

Also I'm enclosing two statements from Mr. Cross who paid me $53.50 today but [is] keeping your part on the books "until you need it"??!?? Did you say anything to them, because both Cross and Andy Tallon were all brimming over with tenderness and benevolence and love to me, and I'm damned if I know what caused the change of heart. I asked Cross if he was sick by any chance and he only giggled, so I can't figure it out for the life of me. Anyway, thank you loads, pop, you're a swell guy and I hereby promise to work any and every Sunday after my bisque to New Bedford this week. And incidentally, if you want me to work on cutting Sir Doakes[2] while I'm away just shoot it back when you send the Irish critic.

Yours, Nowell

1. Katharine S. White (Mrs. E. B. White) of the *New Yorker*. In a letter to the editor of the *New York Times Book Review*, February 5, 1961, she recalled the circumstances surrounding the publication of "Mr. Malone."

2. Part of the "Doaksology," a comic treatment of the various ancestors of Joe Doaks, the protagonist of a new Wolfe novel to be called *The Life and Times of Joseph Doaks*.

❧   ❧   ❧   114 East 56th Street
                                    New York
                                    March 29, 1937

Dear Wolfe:

Herewith the third and last check from the New Republic for
I HAVE A THING TO TELL YOU. It came to $106.86 this time and
I've deducted the typing charge for "Mr. Malone"—$3.98, as well
as my 10%—which leaves $92.14. No more now as I'm hastening
down to see Dagliesh at Scribner's and apologize to Mr. P. for my
dereliction last night. See you soon.

                              Yours, Nowell

P.S. Just dropped into Colliers. Littauer[1] was closeted with some big
shot but I saw his assistant Miss Bouteele kind of casually. She said
she thought the Child by Tiger was terribly swell but doubted if
Colliers dared get away with it. But that Littauer still had it and she
thought "he was showing it proudly to all his friends" (which is what
he does when he likes a story). She said she didn't think it would be
much longer but I said not to rush him in case he might buy it. So I
guess we'd better leave it like that for now.

Mr. P. pretended to be mad but really wasn't and insisted on asking
me "How *is* Rob anyway." (The old joke). He seemed fairly doubtful
about this anthology business about "The Far and the Near" when I
explained it was for the Modern Age[2] bunch who are going to sell
mostly on news-stands and by mail order, so I said I wouldn't do
anything about it now but would wait and see. Yrs.

                              EN

1. Kenneth Littauer, fiction editor of *Collier's* magazine.
2. A left-wing publishing house. Wolfe's story did not appear in the anthology.

❧   ❧   ❧   114 East 56th Street
                                    New York
                                    April 8, 1937

Dear Wolfe:

Here it is at last, 1500 dollars from Redbook minus $150 for me,
leaving $1350. And I hope you won't forget to deposit this one, or
I'll die of joy and surprise when my balance comes out wrong next
month.

I finally got Mrs. White's secretary on the phone and she said she
was coming back on Monday. So I said OK, but not to hurry her in
case she wanted to give any special deep thought or such to "Mr.

Malone." Still no word from Collier's, but sit tight and don't worry about it, you never can tell.

> Yrs, Nowell

❧   ❧   ❧

[carbon copy]

Roanoke, Virginia
April 28th, 1937

Dear Miss Nowell:

I am enclosing a letter to Mr. Palmer of the Mercury. He wrote me about a month ago but since I have written no letters in the past month or so, this is the first chance I have had to reply to him.

He spoke to me about joining the Players' Club,[1] which I do not want to do but which I am trying to evade gracefully. He also spoke to me about getting another piece for the Mercury, which, of course, I am all for if we have anything which suits him.

I can't remember whether his first name is Paul or not and I don't know where the Mercury is now located, except that it is somewhere in Connecticut, so I am just saying "Dear Mr. Palmer" et cetera and leaving it to you to supply the address and send the letter on to him.

I am feeling a lot better except for a terrible feeling of guilt at having loafed so. I have begun to sleep again. In fact, it's about all I am doing nowadays and I am beginning to worry about that too. We can't be satisfied, can we? I feel like working again. I did over two thousand words yesterday and a thousand this morning. I am boiling over with ideas and in short, I believe everything is going to be all right in a few days.

I am going from here down to Bristol, Virginia, and from there over to Yancey County, North Carolina, where my Mother's people are from. I am dreading Asheville a little but I think I will be ready for it in a few days.[2] After that I will be back at work again. I don't know where to tell you to reach me. If anything turns up, I suppose the best address is in care of my Mother, Mrs. Julia E. Wolfe, 48 Spruce Street, Asheville, N.C.

I was awfully glad to hear that the New Yorker took the piece and I hope we will have some luck with the Tiger piece[3] for the Redbook. If they don't want it, maybe you could try Palmer after you have tried the Post. This is all for the present.

The weather has been rotten for several days but is beautiful today and everything is bursting out. This is a nice town with the mountains around it—very much like Asheville.

I had to go to the bank this morning and they wanted some one to identify me. I met some very nice people here and am staying over until tomorrow.

Goodbye for the present. I will be ready to go again when I get back. Meanwhile, with all good wishes,

Ever yours
Thomas Wolfe

1. Paul Palmer had offered to sponsor Wolfe for membership in the Player's Club.
2. Wolfe feared that there would still be some animosity toward him. When *Look Homeward, Angel* was published, he had even received one letter threatening his life if he ever returned to Asheville.
3. "The Child by Tiger."

114 East 56th Street
New York
May 5, 1937

Dear Wolfe:

Maybe this will make you sore because I promised not to bother you [in Asheville], but Mrs. White was terribly insistent on her haste to get galleys back and Perkins and I thought that you really ought to see the piece yourself and make the changes necessary in your own words.[1]

I think Mrs. White's letter is self explanatory, except for a few things; first of all, what she says about it's being all right to have the man in his early forties since he is now fifty years old. I called her up on the phone and pointed out that the phrase "of that lost day and time" made him not forty now but forty about ten years ago. So we decided we had better take out that phrase and just let it go as if it were the present. The chief thing for you to do is to write in a phrase making him denounce Mr. Boyd along with all the other writers—pooh-poohing him also on galley four. Also to change the part on galley five where he says that he lived in Dublin and knew him intimately for forty years. Ernst[2] says that this is the most dangerous part of the whole thing and it is much better not to mention Dublin at all, since Boyd might prove that he was the only critic in the U.S. who had come from Dublin.

Well I guess this is all, except to repeat that we do hope you can send the galleys back and I'm enclosing an air mail stamped envelope so you won't have to go to the trouble of finding one and all that sort of thing. Will hold the check here until you come back unless you need it—in which case I'll send it down. Incidentally, I'd better explain why these marks on the galleys are in my writing instead of Mrs. White's. They are word for word what she wrote on the reader's set but because we are not sure of reaching you she gave me this second set and asked me to transfer her remarks so that the reader's set would be sure not to get lost. As long as I am writing I may as well enclose these letters from Collier's and Redbook and Palmer. THE CHILD BY TIGER is now at Saturday Evening Post so don't worry and have a good time—in spite of my picking on you.

Yours, Nowell

PS: When I read it over I discovered that they had already made him mention Boyd on galley six—which I gather will do instead of having him denounce Boyd on galley four.   EN

1. Because Marjorie Dorman had sued Wolfe for libel over his unfavorable portrayal of her in the story, "No Door," Mrs. White and others feared a law suit if Ernest Boyd recognized himself in the character, "Mr. Malone." As a consequence, she wanted several details altered.

2. Morris Ernst, the lawyer for the *New Yorker*, suggested having Mr. Malone denounce Ernest Boyd along with several other well-known critics for their poor taste and judgment.

❦ ❦ ❦   May 11, 1937

Thomas Wolfe
Care Mrs. Julia E. Wolfe
48 Spruce St.
Asheville N. Car

NEW YORKER SCHEDULED MALONE FOR ISSUE GOING TO PRESS THIS WEEK   LAWYER SAYS PROOF OKAY AS IS WITH NO MORE FIXING ABOUT DUBLIN OR ANYTHING   WILL YOU JUST WIRE ME OKAY MALONE SO THEY CAN GO AHEAD

NOWELL

❦ ❦ ❦   [May 12, 1937]

Thomas Wolfe
Care of Mrs. Julia Wolfe 48 Spruce Street Asheville N Car

I CANNOT POSSIBLY TAKE RESPONSIBILITY ON ANYTHING AS TICKLISH AS MALONE WITHOUT YOU READING IT   HAVE PERSUADED NEW YORKER TO WAIT UNTIL TOMORROW BUT IF NOT OKAYED BY THEN THEY DOUBT CAN USE AT ALL DO PLEASE READ PROOF IMMEDIATELY AND WIRE ME   IT WILL TAKE ONLY TEN MINUTES

NOWELL

❦   ❦   ❦   114 East 56th Street
                              New York
                              May 18, 1937

Dear Wolfe:

Herewith the New Yorker dough. $400 minus my $40. With love and a deep sigh of relief,

                              Nowell

❦   ❦   ❦   114 East 56th Street
                              New York
                              May 20, 1937

Dear Wolfe:

Herewith the dough from Saturday Evening Post minus mine and with hopes for many more.

                              Love, Nowell

❦   ❦   ❦   114 East 56th Street
                              New York
                              June 20, 1937

Dear Wolfe:

Whew! I can't seem to get it[1] under 10892 words, and it may be that I've cut too much in places because I got kind of desperate at the end. But anyway you look at it and see what you think. If necessary I s'pose we could take out that swell passage about the Berengaria's sailing, but it's so swell that I can't bear to do it.

Well, anyway, read it over and see what you think. I'm enclosing the quote from "The Killers"[2] so you can see what to change if you think anything needs changing in that part. And I guess the only other thing is for you to see whether you want to make George think about rivers, hearts, etc. when he's looking at the picture instead of describing him objectively there, which it really doesn't need??

Guess this is all, but cheer up, comrade, because the end is almost in sight.

                          Yrs.   Nowell

P.S. I started to send April Late April[3] to Palmer but decided to ask him about price first. So have dispatched what I think is a very Machiavellian note saying that the big mags have raised you to $2000 but that you still want to write mostly for quality group & *if* he can give you more than $260 I *think* I can persuade you to polish up "The German Girl" story[4] before you leave instead of writing another story for Post.

1. "No More Rivers."

2. The two gangsters in Hemingway's story, "The Killers," exchange a joke about a "kosher convent." Wolfe had something similar in "No More Rivers," which Nowell suggested he remove because she thought it smacked of "plagiarism."

3. Published in the *American Mercury*, September 1937.

4. When he was in Germany, Wolfe had some difficulty taking his German girl friend, Thea Voelcker, across the Austrian border for a holiday. He saw the basis of a story in this experience and began to sketch it out. See *The Notebooks of Thomas Wolfe*, edited by Richard S. Kennedy and Paschal Reeves (Chapel Hill: University of North Carolina Press, 1970), pp. 826–27, for the opening paragraphs. Wolfe never finished it.

❦   ❦   ❦   [Letter fragment, from Wolfe to Nowell, July 1937, from Asheville, North Carolina.]

[carbon copy]
Miss Elizabeth Nowell
114 East 56 Street
New York City
Cont.

reason why I should not be able to settle down to work here and get a great deal done this summer.

I haven't decided yet what I am going to do about New York, or my apartment, or the belongings I have left there. Between now and October, of course, I will have to make a decision and probably a trip back to New York to pack up my remaining possessions. Meanwhile I hope you keep me informed on the news and, of course I hope we manage to sell the remaining stories.

I'll write you again and let you know the progress I am making when I get back to work. I hope you are surviving the weather in New York and will not work too hard. It has been warm for several days, but the nights are always cool and it is a wonderful place to sleep.

Good by for the present, I hope to hear from you soon, meanwhile with all good wishes.

Yours,

❦   ❦   ❦   114 East 56th Street
New York
July 7, 1937

Dear Wolfe:

In case you're beginning to be afraid I've dropped dead, I guess I'd better assure you that everything is OK and you have about $700 coming to you: $300 for April Late April and $400 for Katamoto[1] to Harper's Bazaar.

Palmer has agreed to keeping April Late April as the title, and has also agreed to leave anthology rights and foreign rights etc. etc. free to you as he should have anyway. I started to deposit the check and mail yours to you but discovered he'd made it out to you instead of me, so have asked him if he'd mind changing it. (I was afraid you might lose it, and to tell you the truth I needed the $30 and didn't know then that the Harper's Bazaar check was going to come along too.) Well, anyway, I'll send it down by to-morrow or the next day, so hope that's OK. And the Harper's Bazaar one is now promised for "in three or four days," so will keep after them for that.

Am enclosing a pretty dumb sort of letter from the great Mr. Stout (Lorimer's successor) at Sat Eve Post.[2] I think the guy is all wrong, but have written him a polite note saying how grateful I was for his criticism and that I would send same down to you but was afraid you wouldn't be able to do anything till fall anyway. So then shall forthwith send it to Redbook and if they buy it I can tell Stout that we couldn't find a way to cut it down and make the telephone ring when George was still in bed, which of course would mean leaving out all the river business and spoiling the whole meaning of the thing. Well, anyway, he meant well and it shows they thought it was pretty good or young Lorimer or Brandt would have sent it back without showing it to Stout, so maybe that will cheer you up and assure you that the SEP is hot for you anyway.

Chickamauga[3] is at American [magazine] so don't worry about that either, because everything is going swell and H's Bazaar is already asking for more stories by you. They wouldn't go to $500 on this, but might on others. And that means you'll get as much from them as from N Yorker but won't have to be pruned way down to please Mrs. White. So now I guess this is all, except to say that I do hope you're happy and getting a good rest and not being driven crazy by too many visitors. No need to answer anything here, but guess that goes without saying.

Love, Nowell

1. Published in *Harper's Bazaar*, October 1937, and later included in Chapter 3 of *You Can't Go Home Again*.

2. Wesley Stout had commented on "No More Rivers": "From page twenty-one, where the telephone rings, Thomas Wolfe has an interesting story, but he is so long in setting his scene that he would not have a quorum left at that point—not in a general magazine, that is."

3. Published in the *Yale Review*, Winter 1938.

❦ ❦ ❦   July 13, 1937
Dear Wolfe:
    Here is the check for APRIL LATE APRIL but it is dwindled
down a little bit because I've deducted the typing bill for NO MORE
RIVERS, which came to eight whole dollars and two cents. And for
KATAMOTO, which came to $3.96. That equals $11.98 in all. Or
258.02 after my commission has come out too.
    The Harper's Bazaar check hasn't come, but I am calling them up
to prod them as soon as it is late enough in the morning for HB
editors to be awake.
    Your girl friend from the Junior League[1] called me up and asked
me to have lunch with her tomorrow. So if there's any gossip worth
reporting you'll hear it anon. However, if she tries to pump me about
you I'll be sphinx-like because God knows I don't know anything
about you and haven't heard.
    But I do hope you're OK in your mountains and nice and cool in
your gabardine suits.
                                Love, Nowell

    1. Sally Saunders.

❦ ❦ ❦   July 16, 1937
[carbon copy]
Miss Elizabeth Nowell
114 East 56th Street
New York City
Dear Miss Nowell:
    I got the check for April Late April ($258.02). Thank you very
much.
    I have begun to work again and think I'll get something done. I'll
let you hear when there is more news.[1]
                                Yours,

    1. Wolfe had by now moved in to a cabin at Oteen, a small mountain community
near Asheville.

❦ ❦ ❦   114 East 56th Street
                                   New York
                                   July 19, 1937
Dear Wolfe:
    Dearie you aren't sick are you? Or is it just because your sister
Mabel[1] has taken you in hand and is answering all your letters? I al-

most fainted when I got two from you—in fact I was almost frightened, thinking there must be some terrific emergency. But all kidding
aside, it was swell to hear from you and know that you are settled
down so well and back at work again. I'm enclosing the check for
KATAMOTO herewith and for once there aren't any lousy little typing charges deducted, because I took them all out of the last check.

CHICKAMAUGA just got turned down by American, alas, and
Perkins is dying to get hold of it for Scribners. But I told him there
were still a few big paying magazines left, so he will have to wait.
I suspect you would rather have it in some other magazine for a
change and I think I'll try Harper's, even at the risk of hurting Perkins' feelings. I have a perfectly good excuse, because Harper's gives
slightly better terms, and you won't be involved in it anyway so don't
worry and I'll let you know what happens later.

There is one thing I wasn't going to bother you with, but if Mabel
is going to keep up your correspondence maybe I might as well: it is
the enclosed letter from Mischa Mindess,[2] and I don't know whether
you will want to get mixed up with him or not. There would be very
little money in it, especially since we would have to split with him for
translating. But if you should want it to appear in Yiddish as some
kind of a patriotic gesture we can do it. In the meanwhile, I wrote
him that you were out of reach until October and asked him to get in
touch with me again at that time if he was still interested. I guess it is
better maybe to let it float until then, though if you are interested in
the idea at all I can consult Perkins, etc.

Well, I guess this is all for now. No word yet from Redbook on NO
MORE RIVERS, but don't worry about anything anyway.

                                        Yours, Nowell

1. Mabel Wheaton, Wolfe's older sister. Nowell is referring to the initials MW on
Wolfe's typewritten letters: his typist was named Martha Wrenshall.
2. A request for permission to translate "I Have a Thing to Tell You" into Yiddish.

❧   ❧   ❧   [ca. July 23, 1937]

[carbon copy]
Miss Elizabeth Nowell
114 E. 56th Street
Dear Miss Nowell:

Thanks for your letter and for the check for Katamoto ($366)
which came yesterday. I am sorry Chickamauga got turned down by
American but after our initial preparation it was not a great surprise.
I thought this story would be the easiest to sell but it is turning out

the hardest. However go ahead and try Harpers if you like and let me know what happens. If Perkins really wants it for Scribners we have always got that to fall back on but it might be a good idea to try the remaining possibilities first. I had so many pieces in Scribners and I really don't think it would hurt to be spread around a little more. I am also willing if necessary to revise the story and perhaps to bring it back more to its original purpose—that is the story of an old man telling about the war and the battle. I think I may have put in a little too much Jim Weaver and his love affair in an effort to make it palatable to the big magazines. I don't feel yet that all of this should be cut out, but I might reduce it and make it play a less important place than it now does.

As to the enclosed letter from Mischa Mindess asking for permission to translate "I Have a Thing to Tell You," I am not so sure. I wouldn't mind at all having it done if it were not for the suggestion of propaganda it might attach to it. And frankly I do not think the story ought to be used in that way. It is a straight story, so far as I know it has no propaganda in it save that that the reader wishes to supply for himself by inference and its greatest value, it seems to me, lies in that fact,—that I wrote it as I wrote all my other stories about a human situation and about living characters. I think it ought to be published and read in that way, and I should be against its being read or used or published in any other way. However, I'll think about it and let you know if I change my mind. Meanwhile, you can handle the matter with your customary diplomacy.

I am working at The Party at Jack's: I have changed and revised it a great deal with an effort to weave it together better and to get it to move more quickly. However, it is bound to be very long, and the problem of finding a market for it is one I'd rather not think about now. If all goes well it may turn out to be a very interesting piece of work; but of course there is the question of its length. However, if I get it in shape I'll send it to you and you can read it over and see what you think.

I think I may have another piece for you that from a commercial point of view may be much more practicable. I put it down in rough draft the other day—it's only an outline yet—but I have called it tentatively "A Great Idea For A Story"—and it might really be that. I got the idea a few days ago from a waiter in Asheville who has been hovering around my table whenever I go in and showing me a great deal of attention. The other day after clearing his throat a good many times and looking cunningly around to make sure that he was in no danger of being overheard and that his priceless secret would be safe he bent over and coyly whispered that he had had in his brain for years "A Great Idea For A Story."[1] It's a little habit waiters have; all of a sudden I thought of at least a dozen of them who in exactly the same way, with the same air of hopeful secrecy, had confided to me that they had a great idea for a story which would make us both a fortune if only a guy like me who knew all the tricks could help him out on it. Of course as a reward for this expert supervision yours truly will get cut in on the profits, movie rights, etc. which will be simply staggering.

Well I composed my soul to patience, put a fixed grin on my face and murmured that I was simply dying to hear it—and you know the rest. You can imagine the kind of stories that they tell—or perhaps you can't. They make Cecil B. DeMille in his most fantastic moments look like a stern realist; this one which he assured me had been given to him by a Greek, a fact which he evidently felt gave it at the outset a sensational value—was all about "A dame in Assyria" and her love affair. She was, the waiter assured me, the richest dame in the country. And her old man used to lock her up on the top floor of her house, which was, the waiter said, thirty stories tall. So help me God I'm not making up a word of this, or even understating it. Well the "guy" comes along then and falls for the dame and climbs up to the thirtieth floor every night to play his banjo to her and to carry on his courtship to her in other ways. The old man dies conveniently and the happy pair are married. The marriage, however, is shortlived. The guy, the waiter said, turns out to be a booze hound— these phrases are the waiter's—begins to stay out late at night, and to run around with a bunch of hot blondes. Finally he deserts her utterly, vanishes in thin air—taking with him a lot of her dough and "joolry." She is still nuts about him, however—apparently they are gluttons for punishment in Assyria—so she hunts for him for the next two years, private detectives, rewards, advertisements in the newspapers and all the rest of it. And then she had "her great idea" —the waiter was really getting warm now. "The dame," he said, "opens up a swell night club, the biggest, swellest night club that anybody ever heard of in Assyria."

And then she puts an ad in the paper informing the public that anyone who comes to her joint the next day will be given a ten-dollar gold piece and as much liquor as they can drink or carry away—"all free for nothing." The waiter cunningly explained the cunning psychology of this move to me. "The dame," he said, "knew that such an ad would inevitably [attract] all the booze hounds in Assyria," including her erring husband. And she was not mistaken. And when she goes downstairs the next morning she finds a line of bar-flies three blocks long, and sure enough there is friend husband, first in line. Well she jerks him out of line right away, tells the cashier to pay off the others but tells husband that she has her suspicions about him, that she doubts whether he is really a genuine bonafide, high grade number one 18-caret Assyrian booze hound. That he will have to come upstairs with her and convince her before she allows him to cash in. Well, he goes with her of course and when she gets into her boudoir, she takes off her veil. The waiter explained to me carefully that the reason the husband didn't recognize her was because she was heavily veiled. Well, I waited and then asked "Then what? What happens then?" and the waiter after giving me a look of great disgust answered, "Then nothing, that's all, she's got him back, see? And isn't it a wow?"

Well now, I got to thinking it all over and decided I might make something of it. And here is my own idea; I had talked with literary waiters of this kind before and always they have some preposterous, fantastic and utterly worthless yarn like this which in some strange way they are all convinced will make them a fortune if only someone like me will help them put it down. Apparently the more far-fetched and preposterous the story, the less it has to do with life, the better it seems to them, simply because, I suppose, it has so little to do with the life that they had seen. And yet they all see so much, they hear so much—the material for a dozen living stories is going on around them all the time, but it never occurs to any of them that anyone would be interested in the real stuff. So that's the way I framed it. I drew upon my experience with a dozen waiters, a hundred restaurants, and let it tell itself. I told what was going on around the waiter all the time that he was talking, the people coming in and out, the other waiter who is a communist and who argues violently for revolution with any customer who will talk with him. The little waitress who has had an illegitimate child a few months before and who has put it in a home and goes to see it every Sunday—in other human things and episodes like this—the whole weave and shift and interplay of life and comedy and tragedy that goes on in a place like this —and all the time the waiter is earnestly telling this preposterous fable—his great idea for a story to the customer.

That's roughly the idea that I had in mind for it—I guess you might call it a kind of study [in] unconscious irony—the stuff of life, the materials for a thousand stories all around one, while someone tells a preposterous fable of far away that never could have happened anywhere. I may revise it and send it on to you. I hope you have some good news soon about No More Rivers. If Red Book turns it down and you think it's worth trying I might try to revise and shorten it to fit the length requirements of The Saturday Evening Post. I'll have to look at it again to find whether I could do it or whether anything of my original story would be left if I cut the twenty pages to four or five to meet Mr. Stout's requirement. At any rate, let me know what happens and what you think about it. I saw " 'E" in the New Yorker[2] but have heard nothing yet of The Post and Red Book stories. Of course I like to get paid for them but it is also nice to have them come out. Goodbye for the present. I'm still hoping things will turn out well here—that is, that I get some work done. I think I shall but I'll let you know when I am more sure about it. Meanwhile, with all the best,

Yours,

1. The following material was developed for Chapter 27 of *You Can't Go Home Again*.

2. " 'E, A Recollection," published July 17, 1937.

114 East 56th Street
New York
July 26, 1937

Dear Wolfe:

Enclosed is a letter from our friend Lee ("cutaway") Hartman,[1] which incidentally, proves that he is one of the dumbest editors of the lot. I felt like sending him a note saying: "Dear Mr. Hartman: Did you ever read a book called WAR AND PEACE?" But have restrained myself for the sake of diplomacy.

Just when I was most disgusted with him your friend Mr. P called up to ask when Nancy Hale's book would be finished, and of course he ended by inquiring after CHICKAMAUGA. So in my sudden revulsion from regular ham editors, I said Well I guessed that he could see it, and sent it down. I gather from your letter that you may be sore about that,[2] and if you don't want them to have it just tell me so and I'll tell him. Of course, if they took it you could revise it to your heart's content because they are used to having you do that and I explained all that to Perkins in my letter. Well, I guess we may as well wait and see what happens but I wanted to apologize and explain and if you want to accuse me of being "a tool of the Scribner interest" I'll take same with humility this time.

I guess you are right about our friend Mischa Mindess, and nothing more will happen until October anyway. So we need not worry about that. But while I'm on the subject of dumb editors, I may as well say that I think Stout was cockeyed about NO MORE RIVERS because the more I think about it the more it seems to me as if what he wanted was a totally different story and it might be easier to try him with some of the new ones, instead of driving you crazy on NO MORE RIVERS. I mean that he wouldn't be able to look at the river and all that very lovely description (which, to my way of thinking, is the best part of the story) would have to come out and the whole point would be changed. In other words, it seems as if Mr. Stout wanted a nice tight little piece about some skirt who called a guy up on the phone, which isn't what you and I were planning.

Well, again, I was one jump ahead of you and got the story back from Redbook and sent it down to Collier's before your letter came. Redbook seemed to think that there was not enough plot in it and the chances are Collier's may too, though I now have Virginia Bird installed as a reader down there and she says that they have been kicking themselves all over the place for turning down CHILD BY TIGER. If you ask me you've done enough work on NO MORE RIVERS and it is better to let me go ahead and sell it, even if it ends up with Harper's Bazaar or some such, instead of your trying to turn yourself inside out on a penny on the chance of satisfying Messrs. Stout.

Incidentally, a very obnoxious youth named Bryan was here from the Post Friday asking for more stories by you. He is that little guy who keeps pestering Perkins and is more of the traveling-salesman-promotion-Darrow[3] kind of guy than anything faintly approaching a critic or editor. However I was very polite to him though I wanted to wring his neck and said that we would probably have more stories in a month or so. He himself admitted that he was just a scout and the stories themselves should go to Brandt or Stout as I've been doing. So don't pay too much attention to this little guy, though I'll nurse him along.

Maybe this all sounds kind of embittered, but it is just because people are so damn dumb. Anyway I think this waiter story sounds terribly swell—both funny and important and—well just plain swell all round. So be sure to remember it if you don't want to write it until you get back and I am glad you're keeping going on THE PARTY AT JACK'S. At the very end of your letter you say: "I'm still hoping things will turn out well here—that is that I get some work done." So I gather you've been getting too much of a rush from the citizens of Asheville. Can't you put a padlock on your gate to your private driveway with a sign saying "Man at Work" or something. Or maybe when it gets too bad you'll just blow off steam in your own inimitable way and then everything will be all right. I do hope so, because it sounds so nice down there that it would be a shame if it didn't work out for you, especially as it is hot and muggy as all hell up here. Maybe you could get started on a great idea for a story or would rather sail ahead on the book. Anyway, I'll leave it up to you.

Guess this is all for now, except that several people mentioned how nice "E" was, so cheer up and for Christ's sake don't worry about CHICKAMAUGA and NO MORE RIVERS, because they will land somewhere yet. Incidentally, you may be wondering why I didn't say anything about your Jr. League girl friend, but to tell you the truth I forgot all about it when I wrote you last. Which goes to show that nothing very exciting happened at lunch. She didn't try to pump me but just babbled along in her own exuberant style and we really had a swell time. It seems she has gone to visit her family for her vacation, so that is one thing you won't have to worry about anyway because they live in Calif.

Yours, Nowell

1. Editor of *Harper's Magazine*.

2. Wolfe had quarreled with Perkins and others at Scribner's because they had persuaded him to settle Marjorie Dorman's libel suit out of court instead of fighting the case. That was the principal reason for his retreat to the North Carolina mountains for the summer.

3. A reference to Whitney Darrow, a vice-president and business manager of Scribner's whom both Wolfe and Nowell disliked because he was more interested in company profits than in high-quality publications.

❧ ❧ ❧   July 29, 1937

[carbon copy]
Miss Elizabeth Nowell
New York City
Dear Miss Nowell:

It looks as if no one's right about Chickamauga except thee and me—and maybe even thee is a little peculiar. Anyway we are finding out something about these great minds that direct the editorial policies of our leading magazines, aren't we? Mr. Hartman's letter was especially refreshing. It is interesting to find out that Scribner's have a strangle-hold upon my "straight fiction," because if I mistake not I have not had a piece of straight fiction in Scribner's for almost three years, and only one of any kind, which was Oktoberfest. Anyway, I'm glad to hear that Perkins has been panting with eagerness to see it and I hope his pants to not cease suddenly after he has read it. As to No More Rivers, I leave the decision as to that in your hands. I doubt that it will be palatable to Collier's and if you get it back you can try with it wherever seems best. I don't mind doing any amount of cutting in the interest of brevity and condensation if it helps to improve the story and does not injure its essential purpose, but if what the Post is driving at is just another boy-and-girl story, I don't see [getting] it to them out of No More Rivers without pretty much destroying everything else in it.

I am going on with The Party at Jack's but it is turning out to be a terrifically complicated and difficult job. But it is a very interesting one, but if I work and weave and rework long and hard enough I may have something very good. The market is a different matter; my plan when I get thru is to have a complete section of the social order, a kind of dense, closely interwoven tapestry made up of the lives and thoughts and destinies of thirty or forty people and all embodied in the structure of the story. It is an elaborate design, it has to be; it is I suppose somewhat Proustian, but this also has to be and the interesting thing about it is the really great amount of action—this action is submerged and perhaps not at first apparent, but if the reader will stick with me, if I can carry him along with me it will be apparent by the time he finishes the story. In spite of all kinds of interruptions— there have been droves of thirsty tourists out here to look at the animal, all the way from a police court judge to the leading hot-dog merchant—I have done a lot of *work* and hope to see where I stand with it in another two weeks. I've enjoyed the social activity but I hope it will slacken down hereafter. I've got to go down to South Carolina over the week and to see my sister but I will be back here working at it Monday.

The weather is fine, the country is beautiful, I am sleeping at night and I think I feel better than when I left New York four weeks ago. My plans for the future are still uncertain. I don't know where I'll be next year or where I'm going to live. All I hope for is to go on with my work and to get something done and to escape somehow the ruinous calamities of the last two years. I may never come back to New York to live and if I do it will be from another angle, with a new plan. But know that I have lived out my young man's experience in New York and I know that I shall not try to continue it. This summer is a halting place, a time to think it over and to decide what I am going to do. I am afraid some of the old connections may be worn out; there are too many scars now, so much disillusionment and disapointment. At any rate, no matter what happens, I hope to go on working and get something done. I am sorry we have had such bad luck with the two stories but I hope to get some good news soon.

Meanwhile, with all good wishes,

Ever yours,

🌷 🌷 🌷   114 East 56th Street
                                    New York
                                    August 16th, 1937.

Dear Wolfe:

I just got back from New Bedford where I was taking time out over the week-end. Dearie, I wouldn't worry about the big magazines at all, if I were you. Don't try to play the slot machine, but just go ahead and write the best you know how, with your eye on Mount Parnassus. If the stories turn out to be possible for the big magazines, then you will be around fifteen hundred berries to the good; but if the big magazines don't know enough to buy them, then you won't have poured out your "heart's blood" for naught.

If you ask me, the big magazines are unpredictable. In fact, I would have said that both the "Lost Boy" and "Child by Tiger" were amongst those stories which were very swell but almost impossible for a big magazine to use. But what do I hear but that the Post is planning to feature you on the cover and make all kinds of hulla-baloo, saying that they expect to lose some of their old readers as a result but they will gain a lot of younger and more intelligent ones.

As for "No More Rivers," it is still at Collier's, although Vi Bird has promised to do all she can to stir it up. Scribner's finally sent back "Chickamauga" with such a confusion of excuses that I'm damned if I know what to say. Perkins felt that it wasn't one of your very best, although when I pinned him down, the only thing I could gather was that he didn't agree with your views on war and that he thought maybe you had done a little too much with the love theme, although he said when I asked him about the Bacchus section, that it really didn't belong in there if the story was going to be a real story. I explained that you had doubts about the love business yourself and would perhaps want to re-write it as more of a narrative, so he took it down to Ives and Logan.[1] Ives liked it very much indeed, although she thought it was pretty long for them (They hold her down quite strictly to 5000) but anyway she gave it to Logan and he found it "pretty hard going." If you ask me, that's the stupidest criticism yet—I suppose he wants things to read as glibly as in Redbook or Cosmo. It sounds as if he didn't appreciate all the salt of the old man's narrative in the least, although maybe I'm being too hard on him. Anyway, he also felt that it was too long—so to hell with them.

George Davis of Harper's Bazaar has been repeating his request for a "great roaring Wolfe story," so I told him what this was about and he said he was very anxious to see it. If you ask me, it's pretty bloody and masculine for a woman's magazine but you never can tell, and if they don't work, we will try your old friend Palmer who called up on Friday when I'd left for home, and said he would 'phone back today. Miss Krainin[2] (Phyllis has departed) said he wanted your address so she gave it to him and I guess the chances are he has written you offering you free membership in the Players, Racquet, and Turf and Fields Club, with perhaps a charter to the Colonial Dames of America—if you will only give him another story. I guess you'd better tip me off to what you write him so that I won't tell any embarrassing lies, or you can just not write him because I've already told him that you never answer letters—not knowing that M.W.,[3] who now seems to have turned into B.E.H.,[4] was going to reform you so completely.

Well, I don't want to ramble on too long, but I do hope that for Christ's sake, you can keep out of that trial,[5] even if it means that you will have to leave N.C. for a while, until it's over. I trust that by this time, you have blown up at Munsterberg so guess that will take care of itself. I haven't been able to get hold of Mrs. Mitchell[6] yet but maybe I will before I mail this, or if not, will write you in a day or two about it. So now I guess this is all for the present.

Yours—Nowell

1. Harlan Logan, editor-publisher of *Scribner's Magazine* and Marian Ives, fiction editor.

2. Ethel Krainin, Nowell's secretary.

3. Martha Wrenshall, Wolfe's typist who came at mid-day every day to his mountain cabin at Oteen, near Asheville, and worked as late as he wished.

4. Martha Wrenshall's replacement, who did not last long because she insisted on working on a nine-to-five schedule.

5. On his first return to Asheville, North Carolina, in April 1937, Wolfe had been a witness in the shooting death of James Higgins, which took place on the streets of Burnsville in Yancey County. He was later called upon to testify in the murder trial.

6. Wolfe's cleaning woman at his New York apartment, 865 First Avenue.

❧ ❧ ❧　　　　114 East 56th Street
New York
August 18th, 1937.

Dear Wolfe:

No word from either you or Crystal[1] yet—although I'm holding my breath in preparation for any emergencies which may come up later in the day. In the meanwhile there are a couple of literary matters that I want to get off my mind, to you.

Collier's finally turned down "No More Rivers" with abject apologies and regrets. It seems that Littauer liked it very much and put it all the way through to Chenery² who is the big shot and finally turned thumbs down. They all thought that it was very fine and very lovely, but used the old excuse that it was too long and didn't get going until after a good many pages. However, it seems to be doing better than we had hoped, so I may as well keep on going and give Cosmopolitan a look. In the meanwhile, Littauer says he would very much like to see you but I explained that you were in Carolina, saying that if you did come back some time this Fall, I would remind you to get in touch with him. It wouldn't prove much one way or another—so you needn't give it another thought—although if you ever are here with a lot of time to kill, you can go and see him if you want to.

In the meanwhile, Balmer sent me proof of "The Lost Boy" with the enclosed note. He called me up first to say that it was coming and said some very nice things about what a fine writer you were and how delighted he was with the story and anxious to have more. Of course, that sounds pretty silly after his having just turned down three, but Balmer is always unpredictable and gets sudden bursts of enthusiasm which are sometimes good for a good deal of dough. I think that when the Post features "Child by Tiger," the other big magazines will be considerably impressed and more apt to buy things —length, or no length. In the meanwhile, I reassured Balmer that none of the names in the "Lost Boy" were of real people and that furthermore Mr. and Mrs. Crockett had both died without issue.

They have what I think is a very swell illustration of the stone cutter confronting Mr. and Mrs. Crockett across the counter. The artist has made him into a sort of idealized and very handsome but still strong looking Abraham Lincoln, and I really think it is a pretty swell picture. There is another full page one of the mother sending the little sister running out for the doctor, so I guess they are going to play it up pretty well. Anyway, it's coming out in the November issue —so you will see for yourself.

There were a few little odds and ends that I questioned, though nothing more serious than slight typographical errors and things of the sort. They left off the Roman numerals at the beginning of the various sections and I said I thought it would be better if they were put back, although if it was dead against their policy, I would cede in the matter.

Well, I guess this is all for now, especially as there might be more later about the rent business.

Love—Nowell

P.S. Miss Krainin just tells me she is not sure whether it was Palmer or Balmer who called the other day. Anyway, I guess it doesn't matter, as long as he got your address.

1. The superintendent of the apartment building at 865 First Avenue, who had not received Wolfe's check for monthly rent.

2. William L. Chenery, editor-in-chief of *Collier's*.

❦   ❦   ❦   [carbon copy of a letter fragment, from Wolfe to Nowell, August 1937, from Asheville, North Carolina]

I've been working on since I came down here. It is still only a draft, but as you will see, in a very much more complete and finished form than what you saw in New York. I have completely re-written it and rewoven it. It was a very difficult piece of work, but I think it is now a single thing, as much a single thing as anything I've ever written. I am not through with it yet. There is a great deal more revision to be done, but I am sending it to you anyway to let you see what I have done and I think you will also be able to see what it may be like when I'm finished with it.

As to the final disposition of it, I do not know. Someone has told me that the thing is a unit in itself and could be, when I am finished with it, published as a unit without further addition. I have not yet made up my mind about this yet.

The whole thing belongs, as you know, to the entire manuscript of The October Fair, of which sections and fragments have been published for years—Death the Proud Brother, April Late April, etc.—and many other things, of course, which have not been published. Mr. Malone, by the way, belongs in the piece that I am sending you, The Party at Jack's, but since Mr. Malone has already been published, I did not think it advisable to include it here. All the other parts which you have seen, the whole long section called Morning—that is, Mr. Jack waking up and feeling the tremor, faint and instant, in the ground beneath him, Mrs. Jack and the maid, the April Late April piece which the Mercury is publishing, the scene in the Station, the long section called The Locusts Have No King, which I do not think you ever saw, Death the Proud Brother, and other matter which perhaps you never read, also belong with this piece. I, therefore, kept a copy and put it all together with some tentative idea in my mind of making a complete book of all of it—a book which would occur within the limits of a single twenty-four hours, beginning from midnight of one day and ending with the midnight of the next and bearing probably the title of The Party at Jack's.

All of this would, of course, be a part of the book that was announced some years ago under the title The October Fair. I have not made my mind up definitely about this yet, but I am sending the manuscript to a friend[1] in New York to get his opinion. As you know, the whole thing has been a very vexed and perturbed part of my writing experience and it has cost me the utmost worry and difficulty because it seemed to me that so much labor, so much effort, and so much that I really think is valuable and good and needs to be saved was in danger of dying the death, of being, in so many various and complicated ways, all of which apparently sprang out of a friend's desire to help you[2] and perhaps some instinctive timidity and caution, suppressed and killed. I cannot say definitely as to all this, but I do know that a man must not be thwarted in the process of his creation and I feel very strongly that this has happened to me with this piece of work.

As to this piece I'm sending you, The Party at Jack's, I feel that whatever else may be said about it, it escapes entirely the objections that were raised about the purpose of The October Fair. I really think that the purpose of The October Fair was misunderstood, and [that] people whose judgment I respected were too quick and willing to assume that the book would be a sequel to the first two books and thus lay me open to the old charges of autobiographic literalness and romanticism, etc., and not as I intended it to be, the progression of my life, the maturing of my experience and my talent. At any rate, The Party at Jack's I believe escapes these feared qualities. I don't believe the charge of "autobiography" can be brought against it, except insofar as they must be brought against the work of any man. I have simply taken the lives of thirty or forty of the people I knew during my years in New York and revealed them during an evening at a party in the city. As to the matter of action it seems to me that the piece is crowded, although perhaps it is not apparently so. But I don't see how any intelligent reader could read it without understanding almost everything that has happened before the piece is ended.

As to the rest of it, the social implications, that I fear would make the piece anathema to almost any of the older publishers, I simply cannot help it. It is simply the way I feel and think, I hope and believe there is not a word of conscious propaganda in it. It is certainly not at all Marxian, but it is representative of the way my life has come after deep feeling, deep thinking, and deep living and all this experience, to take its way. And I believe and hope, also, that this piece will show the energy of life, a genuine and reverent love of life and a spirit of understanding and compassion for all the characters. I hope and believe that it has passion in it, indignation and denunciation and I hope also it has pity and love and comprehension in it.

You are seeing the thing in its first blocking out: if all these qualities, and I hope for it, are not fully revealed now, I hope they will be when I get through working on it. It is in concept at any rate the most densely woven piece of writing that I have ever attempted. There is not much more that I can tell you about it except that I wish you would read it as it is, in and for itself without too much reference to these other portions I have mentioned, of which it is also a part. But just read it, if you can, as a story in itself and see if you think it carries the unity and direction of a single thing. Because I am not certain that I shall be here more than a day or two longer, I am sending you the piece in its present unrevised and uncorrected form. Traveling around with great bags of manuscript—and I've written sixty or eighty thousand words since I came down here—is a precarious business, and I would like to know that, even in its present form, you have a copy in your hands. Another copy will be in the keeping of a friend in New York and I hope to keep the final one intact for myself.

It's pretty hard to tell you what I shall do about staying here in Asheville. I wanted to come back, I thought about it for years. I think I shall like still to stay and work if it were possible. As you know, I have never put much stock in looking for "places to work." It seems to me that a man can work almost any place he wants to. But my stay here this summer has really resembled a three-ringed circus. I think people have wanted to be and have tried to be most kind, but they wore me to a frazzle. My cabin outside of town was situated in an isolated and quite beautiful spot, but they found their way to it and in addition I found out that it is, to say the least, terribly difficult to keep a Negro servant in such a place. They are afraid of the dark. That is about what it amounts to. As a result, they were always disappearing at night and not coming back until the next morning. When I had to go to Burnsville the other day to the murder trial, the boy I had at the cabin disappeared and didn't show up again for three or four days. Then he said that he was frightened to stay there by himself at night alone and would like to quit. Of course it's not their fault but just the way they are.

As to living in town here, I don't know whether that can work out or not. I know so many people here and the place is really very small. People know everything you do, even before you do it—it's always that way isn't it—and they are still, in a friendly way, living over the whole vexed experience of Look Homeward Angel and of having the culprit back in their midst. It is a beautiful country here. I shall always miss it, but perhaps what I had thought possible cannot happen.

At any rate, the summer has not been lost. I have established the connection again and, of course, completed gathering all the materials for perhaps the most tragic incidents of our collapse, of what happened to the entire nation, in the history of the country. I don't think anything else like it could be found: the whole thing intensified and specialized is here.[3] And since it is my own home place, of course, I have the deepest interest, the profoundest sympathy with all of it.

I may go up to Virginia for a day or two to see Sherwood Anderson. As to mailing addresses for the present I don't know what to tell you. I still have my cabin at Oteen until September and I am still trying to think my way through this, to find out what I am going to do. I think for the present if you would send any communication you may have to General Delivery, Asheville, N.C., that would be the quickest and safest address. Then if there is any change I can leave word there where the mail should be forwarded. This is all for the present, and too much as usual. Please let me know if you receive the manuscript of The Party at Jack's safely, and what, if any, you think the prospects are.

Meanwhile, with thanks and all good wishes,

Sincerely,

1. Wolfe perhaps refers to Henry Volkening, a former colleague at New York University whose judgment he respected and who later became a literary agent.

2. Perkins had been apprehensive about Wolfe's going ahead on The October Fair because it drew upon Wolfe's love affair with Aline Bernstein, and Mrs. Bernstein had threatened to sue if Wolfe wrote about her. As a result, he advised Wolfe to work on other parts of the Eugene Gant cycle and encouraged him to undertake the new project, The Vision of Spangler's Paul.

3. Wolfe refers to the economic collapse in Asheville, which was attended by bank failures, misappropriation of civic funds, and the bursting of a real estate bubble. He had in mind that the Asheville experience was a paradigm of the national situation, and he intended to use it for social criticism in his fiction. Although this plan was never completed, parts of it appear in Chapters 7, 8, 9, and 25 of You Can't Go Home Again.

114 East 56th Street
New York
August 23rd, 1937.

Dear Wolfe:

Just a line in haste to reassure you that the check is on its way to Crystal and everything OK.

Perkins and I were so afraid that they would really dispossess you that he had already started a check down to them but we were able to retrieve it when I got yours just now.

"The Party at Jack's" hasn't come yet but I guess it will take a little longer since it's a big manuscript. Anyway, don't worry and I'll guard it with my life and read it with great eagerness. I can't quite make out where you are going to be but guess you don't know yourself—so will be writing you about "The Party at Jack's," care of general delivery.

I won't say any more now because I want to get this off tonight, without fail. Maybe if Asheville doesn't work out, you can try some place in Connecticut,[1] which would be near New York but out of all the tumult. However, I guess you will figure that all out for yourself and I certainly am relieved that the trial was no worse.

Have a good time and don't worry about anything.

Yours—

1. Wolfe had considered leaving New York and settling in Asheville, but he was so badgered by visitors to his secluded mountain cabin at Oteen that he had now moved into the Battery Park Hotel in Asheville for privacy in which to work.

95 Madison St.
New Bedford, Mass.
Sunday [September 1937]

Dear Wolfe:

This is Sunday, but I've just finished The Party at Jack's and wanted to write you right off to say what a swell job it was. Of course I'd already read a good deal of it and knew that much was swell anyway, but all the way through this time I kept getting little shocks of pleasure to see what you'd done to improve it, and all those swell satiric or emotional touches you'd added and everything. I guess there's no doubt about it that the longer and deeper you go into things the sweller they come out. And what's more you've got a damn near perfect critical sense for rounding things out.

All of this is written in just a general enthusiasm for the thing as a piece of work, and how it will work for a magazine I don't know yet, because I'm still too close to it and full of it to have got coldly ana-

lytical about chopping passages out, making all those nasty little
brackets etc. etc. So I can't tell how short I could get it without
ruining it until I mull it over and fiddle around for a good while.
There's one thing that I sort of miss to cut down to, and I can't make
out whether you mean it to go in or not. On the phone that day you
said something about the section about Mr. J getting up in the morning's belonging in it, and I do think it would be a good idea to
introduce him earlier instead of having him not really amount to
anything until Piggy is jamming the sword into the doll's entrails. It
wouldn't necessarily have to be in the morning, I should think, but
could show him getting dressed in his own room a little after Mrs.
Jack first looks around before the party or somewhere in there.
Somehow I think that would plant the seed better for the last section
of all when he is going to bed and hears the rumble of the train,
which is swell and symbolic and well, just damn near perfect all
around.

Well, I guess you were thinking of using it if you do use this as a
book as you might well do, especially if some of the people you
telephoned to are anxious to publish something right away[1] so you
can get it settled and off your chest, as I guess would be a great relief
to you. Or did you mean to work this into the big Doaks book as one
unit, which God knows would also be swell and perfectly possible.
Well, all of this is just thinking out loud and none of my business,
and even if you did need this copy just as it stands to show to
somebody when you come north, we could get it copied over even if
I have made nasty little brackets on some of it by then. Right this
minute my brain feels stale and dead as last year's catch of fish, so I
won't be doing anything until I really feel ready and clear and right
about what I'm going to do. Maybe it will finally convince me that it
won't cut down enough and I'd better not do it for fear of ruining it,
but I do think there are some big sections that I might be able to take
out wholesale, like some of the minor characters at the party or
conversations or something which would drag too much for a magazine although of course I know what they prove and why you want
them for the really complete piece.

I'm afraid this is a pretty vague and puzzling letter, but all I meant
to write was how swell I thought is was. So I'll be trying to figure out
the rest and have more definite word for you by the time you either
show up in NY or settle down somewhere with a more permanent
address. So if you want anything just call me up or write me and I'll
try to give you the best advice, help, or anything I possibly can. As
long as you're such a swell writer you can't possibly be "knifed" or

fail in any way, because you just plain *are* and no matter how people may worry or irritate you, you're bound to come through all right by sheer talent and genius and sincerity. Oh lord, I can see you grinning ruefully to yourself and answering "That's all right, sister, but. . . ." and maybe I sound like some kind of sappy Pollyanna. But I really believe it will come out all right in the end, although I admit you may have to go through considerable hell in the meanwhile. So take it easy and let me know when and if you want anything, and you really and truly can trust me, I promise.

Yrs, Nowell

1. From Asheville, Wolfe had telephoned several New York publishing houses inquiring if they had the desire to publish his novels.

PART VI ❧ November 1937 to March 1938
Wolfe Chooses a New Publisher

*Back once more in New York, Wolfe spent the fall in negotiations
with publishers, a period that ended in a contract with Harper and
Brothers and association with a young editor, Edward Aswell, a
Southerner who had been an enthusiastic follower of all Wolfe's
published work.*

*Wolfe by now had turned to a new novel, indulging himself in
the creative therapy of social criticism and satire on the New York
literary life. His new alter ego was a bumbling anti-hero, named
appropriately Joe Doaks. Wolfe placed this character at the center of
his ever-lengthening short novel, "The Party at Jack's," and very
gradually his adventures began to take over material that had been
intended for "The Vision of Spangler's Paul." The contract that he
signed with Harper in December 1937 gave the title of this novel as
"The Life and Times of Joseph Doaks."*

*Yet, as he began to prepare a narrative sequence for the book in
order to fulfill his contract, Wolfe gradually amalgamated all of the
autobiographical episodes he had been writing about Paul or George
Spangler and Joseph Doaks with the material that remained about
Eugene Gant. He renamed his hero George Webber and assembled
every item he could conceivably integrate into his story line.*

*The narrative began with an account of George's maternal ances-
tors, the Joyners, in the Appalachian region and the arrival of his
father, John Webber, in the town of Libya Hill. It went on to the
story of George Webber's childhood in Libya Hill, his yearning to
visit the North where his father had come from, his friendships and
education during his college years, his travel to New York for a teaching job, his desire to become a novelist, his love affair with a New
York stage designer, his achievement of success and fame as a novelist, his adventures in various European countries, and his arrival at a
maturity of outlook on life, a point at which he realized that love and
fame were meaningless unless he could understand himself and control his divided impulses. Webber also came to see that his life had
changed irrevocably, that it was impossible for him to go back to the
former life of his youth and his region, that his past was only signifi-
cant for him if he could draw upon it for disciplined artistic growth.*

❦ ❦ ❦   114 East 56th Street
                                           New York
                                           November 3, 1937

Dear Wolfe:

A guy named Mr. Gercke just called up, who is in charge of distribution of department of agriculture films and asked you to a preview of one of their pictures[1] tomorrow at 6 o'clock at the Preview Theatre, 1600 Broadway, between 48th and 49th. (Tomorrow being Thursday.) It seems that when you were at Arnaud's in New Orleans you met a very good photographer named Willard Van Dyck and in talking with him said that you had never seen a picture about real America or anything decent of that sort. Well, evidently Van Dyck has remembered it all this time because he is the one who suggested asking you, though he was out of town today with Pare Lorenz, who is also mixed up in the agricultural picture-making. Gercke sounded like quite a nice guy and explained that they had been showing it to critics and columnists, etc. but I don't *think* there's any catch to this like asking you to make a statement after you've seen it because he said that you could just walk in and sit down and watch it and nobody would bother you, though if you wanted to ask for him when you got there he would be there. He also said that they would be showing it from time to time for the next week, then taking it off and fixing it, and finally, I guess, getting it into shape for the general public. But that anyway if you couldn't make it Thursday and wanted to see it any other time, just to give him a ring at Vanderbilt 3–4676 and he would tell you the best times etc.

So now I guess this is all. If you've just got going on work I guess you'll want to skip it, but I thought it might come in handy as a way to keep The Polings[2] out of mischief or something so [I thought] I'd tell you anyway.

                                    Yrs   Nowell

P.S. I asked Gercke what it was about and he said floods and things like that.

1. "The River."

2. At this time, Wolfe was engaged in discussions of a prospective publishing agreement with James Poling, managing editor of Doubleday and Company.

114 East 56th Street
New York
November 4th, 1937

Dear Wolfe:

Just a line to say that Perkins just called up to say that your New Jersey lawyers (!)[1] had sent him a letter saying that they were very anxious to get in touch with you and would you communicate with them. In case you don't know, their names as I got it over the telephone are:

Lum, Tamblyn & Fairlie
605 Broad Street

And Perkins seemed to think that they were really getting somewhere, though he admitted that they didn't say what was up in this letter, since it was just asking for your address. I will mail their letter down when I get it from him tomorrow, but he wanted me to be sure that I got the word right down to you.

Speaking of lawyers, I enclose another note from your friend Mr. Kane[2] and various other letters for you and Mrs. Wolfe???? No word from McAfee[3] but I think we will hear very soon.

Yours, Nowell

1. Because Murdach Dooher lived across the river in New Jersey, Wolfe needed a firm of New Jersey lawyers to conduct his lawsuit against Dooher.
2. Melville Cane, the lawyer who had drawn up Wolfe's will.
3. Helen McAfee of the *Yale Review*, who was reading "Chickamauga."

114 East 56th Street
New York
November 5, 1937

Dear Wolfe:

Perkins just made his daily call to say that he had just got a postcard from your mother saying that she hadn't heard from you since October 4th—something about she didn't like to bother you but it made her ashamed for you when people asked her how you were and she couldn't tell them. Well, anyway, I told him to mail it up to me so I could send it to you to see for yourself, but I think he's going to answer her anyway in the meanwhile, just to reassure her; and if you want me to do likewise until you get a chance to drop her a line, just let me know.

Yours, E N

❧ ❧ ❧   114 East 56th Street
                                 New York
                                 November 5, 1937

Dear Wolfe:

Here is the dirt I got from Mr. Hull, the conductor, translated from my hurried pencil notes that I showed you the other day.

He says that that fire was at 270 Park Ave. on Jan. 3, 1930,[1] and that the root of the fire was in the sub-cellar of the building. Said sub-cellar was underneath two levels of track in the Grand Central train yard, upper and lower level. Accordingly, the firemen had to go down through two gratings in the tracks to get into the sub-cellar to fight the fire. The track he mentions specifically as being made impossible for traffic was track #132, though I guess there must have been another one on the lower level which he didn't give me the number of. Anyway, I gather that they had not actually flooded the tracks but couldn't have trains running over them because of the firemen popping in and out of the gratings with chemicals, hose, etc. etc.

                                 Yours, Nowell

1. In "The Party at Jack's," Wolfe was writing about the fire in the apartment building that took place during a party given by Mr. and Mrs. Bernstein.

❧ ❧ ❧   114 East 56th Street
                                 New York
                                 November 10, 1937

Dear Mr. Vulfe:

It seems that Ed Aswell[1] at Harper's has just heard the "rumors" that you are free of C.S.S. You know, he's the one that I said I knew was honest, that you met with his wife at a party once, and who is a personal friend of mine. He is Saxton's[2] assistant and one of the few people that I really trust, because even if Harper's is like any publisher, maybe sometimes even more penny-pinching, Ed has always done what was fair by the one Harper book-author I have. Well, I guess you remember my telling you about him and saying that I knew he'd jump at the chance if you wanted to tell him, but you said you'd talked on the phone with Hartman,[3] so that was that. I swear by all that's holy or something that I never let out so much as a peep to him, but this afternoon around five oclock he called up out of a clear sky and said he'd heard "the rumors" and asked me if it was true. I told him that it was and that he could write you in my care and I'd forward it to you special (I didn't say whether you were in NY or not, but used the old line about you hadn't settled down anywhere) and he said OK, he'd write you but would I write you in the meanwhile to-night so as not to lose any time.

He was sort of hurt and reproachful that I hadn't told him before, especially that time I was out at their house in Pleasantville for dinner a couple of weeks ago, so I explained that part to him—that I had told you there was nothing I thought he'd like better than to hear about it, but that you had said you'd talked with Hartman though I didn't know what the outcome of the conversation was. I also explained that I didn't really know what plans you had because I had nothing to do with your books, and I didn't say anything about Houghton Mifflin[4] because I figured that would be telling more than I was sposed to.

So now I guess this reproduces the whole telephone conversation play by play, and I hope it won't be too much of a bother for you. I'll forward his letter down when it comes, but I promise not to tell Ed anything and to keep out of the whole business.

Yrs, Nowell

1. Edward Aswell, an assistant editor at Harper and Brothers, who later arranged a contract for Wolfe's next book.

2. Eugene Saxton, the senior editor at Harper and Brothers.

3. When Wolfe had telephoned several New York publishers from Asheville, asking if they would like to publish his work, his telephone call to Harper and Brothers was connected by mistake to *Harper's Magazine*, where he talked with the editor, Lee Hartman. Hartman misunderstood Wolfe's question, thinking that he was asking if they were interested in publishing his stories in the magazine; so he casually told Wolfe to send his material along and they would consider it. Wolfe was offended by this treatment and refused to allow Nowell to speak to anyone else at Harper and Brothers about his desire to change publishers.

4. Wolfe was currently engaged in contract discussions with Robert N. Linscott of Houghton Mifflin.

114 East 56th Street
New York
November 16, 1937

Dear Wolfe:

Herewith a little item from your friends the New Jersey lawyers, and my answer to them, which I hope is O.K. Also, a couple of other interruptions from Sally[1] and Fred[2] and a note from Miss McAfee about the title of Chicamauga. I guess we will have to give in to her on this and I am sorry, but don't pay any attention because I will just write her O.K.

Yours, Nowell

1. Sally Saunders.
2. Wolfe's older brother.

❦   ❦   ❦   114 East 56th Street
                                       New York
                                       November 18, 1937

Dear Wolfe:

Just a line to reassure you that if and when Miss Boie[1] arrives in town all full of school teacher ideas of telling you how and what to write, you will have left on a hypothetical trip to Tierra del Fuego (sp?) or some such. And also to explain that the top part of one letter which I cut off was nothing to you but about a story of Elick Moll's which I had to send to him.

I promised you I'd tell you if No More Rivers came back from the Atlantic or otherwise would just go ahead with it, but I *don't* think you ought to take your mind off your book to fiddle around with it for the Post now, do you, unless you are really very broke? I guess I would normally try it with either Harper's or Harper's Bazaar next, but maybe you wouldn't want me to send it down to Harper's, not because it isn't swell but for fear they might think they'd have to take it because of the other business or something. Well, you know, I guess maybe that's false delicacy and for all I know it may be a good idea to send it there to try them out, though Hartman and the magazine hasn't got much to do with Aswell, and Canfield[2] and Co. But at any rate, I guess I shouldn't go rushing in where maybe you wouldn't want me to until I find out how it strikes you. Although on the other hand, Canfield may have suggested that you show the magazine some stories for all I know. Well, what the hell, I seem to have not got very much involved here imagining all kinds of fine shades of diplomacy and what-not. We still have the whole "quality magazine" field to try except for the Atlantic: Mercury, Harper's Bazaar, etc. etc. So I guess I'll just hold it here till you give me a ring some time, though I'm going away Friday for Thanksgiving (a whole week!!) but Miss Krainin will forward all mail every day as before, and will phone me at a minute's notice if you want to talk to me for anything.

Otherwise no mail for you today, no lawyers no nothing, so may they rest in peace.

                                       Yrs, Nowell

1. Mildred Boie was an assistant editor of the *Atlantic Monthly*, who had been reading "No More Rivers."
2. Cass Canfield was the president of Harper and Brothers.

🌷 🌷 🌷

114 East 56th Street
New York
December 3, 1937

Dear Wolfe:

I didn't have the heart to read this to you to-night because I knew you were upset enough about other things as it was. But I know I ought to show it to you, and I think it's better to send it down to-night than to have you get it Monday and have it break in on a good day's work. Not that it's anything serious, but maybe you'll worry over what reason she has if any for not wanting you to write her, or some such.[1]

Maybe I shouldn't have stuck in that line about "He will probably be writing you himself when he receives them, but in case he's slow in doing so, I want to try to explain." I asked you if it was OK on the phone and you said yes, and I honestly do think it was necessary to make plausible by writing all of that when there was no reason for me to write her at all. . . . Oh well, what the hell, I'm writing all of this now because I'm so self-conscious for fear you might think I'd "talked too much" or something like that to Mrs. B in my letter.

I really am so sorry and ashamed about what you said about my chattering to Perkins that time years ago,[2] but it will do no harm for me to be ashamed, and will maybe help me remember to keep my mouth shut better in future emergencies or temptations. But I wish the hell people would stop calling me up and taking me out or cornering me at Scribner's and trying to pump me about you, because whatever I say may either be wrong or be misinterpreted or repeated wrong, or something of the sort. And if I say "I can't answer that" or "I have nothing to say" it sort of makes people think that there is something dark and mysterious which I'm hiding from them. Well, anyway, I think I'll try harder to repeat that you don't like me to chatter about you, both to Scribner's if I see any of them and also to Ed and the Houghton Mifflin bunch if they swoop down on me. Maybe this sounds as if I was trying to dodge or rationalize what you said, and I'm not. In fact I admit that I always used to talk too much and still slip up now and then, even though I honestly am trying to learn not to. So it will do no harm for you to remind me of it once in a while, drunk or sober, or any other way, and I honestly would appreciate same as long as I know you aren't harboring any suspicions against me. So now I guess this is all, but you call me whenever you feel like [about] the Vogue piece,[3] or any other time.

Yrs   Nowell

1. Aline Bernstein had written to Nowell telling her that she had found some of

Wolfe's family photographs and wished to send them to him. Nowell was now sending Wolfe a copy of her reply to Mrs. Bernstein.

2. Nowell had ridiculed a passage in Wolfe's short novel, "No Door," about the narrator's "beating his bloody knuckles on the wall" and Perkins had repeated her remarks to Wolfe.

3. Allene Talmey of *Vogue* magazine had taken Wolfe to tea at the Colony Restaurant in order to discuss with him his making a contribution to their planned "Americana" issue. This invitation led to Wolfe's construction of "Prologue to America" out of the opening portion of his manuscript, "The Hound of Darkness."

❦ ❦ ❦   114 East 56th Street
                                       New York
                                       December 9, 1937

Dear Wolfe:

I guess this will make you feel better—$112.50 from the Yale Review for "Chickamauga" which represents $125 minus $12.50 for yours truly. The author's copies of it just came and I'll mail one down to you by second-class mail or however it is that magazines go.

Also enclosed, a raft of letters, including a postcard from Fred. I'm writing him to say that you did get the neckties and the nuts O.K., so you won't have to rush to answer him.

Yours, Nowell

P.S. The article went down to Vogue this morning, so keep your fingers crossed.

P.S. Enclosed latest phone message with no comment, rush, in case you want to discuss? with EN & G.[1]

1. Elizabeth Nowell and perhaps Mike Gold, the editor of *New Masses*, whom Wolfe had recently met and to whom he sent his story, "The Company," which was published in *New Masses*, January, 11, 1938.

❦ ❦ ❦   Christmas Eve

Dear Wolfe:

I've always wanted one,[1] and I can't for the life of me remember if I told you how I loved them when we were talking about Germany or whether it was just luck that you saw it and liked it too. As a matter of fact I used to walk down Madison at night to get Marshal Ney[2] out of my head before going to bed and gawk at this very same angel or one like it in Rene R's side window. But my N. England tightfistedness would never let me go back in the daytime to buy one, so there isn't anything in the world I'd get more of a sentimental kick out of having for a real Christmas. She's up in front of the clock on my desk now, and there she stays forever and ever. I've tried phoning you a couple of times since it got here but I guess you're out celebrating somewhere and I'm afraid you'll either be asleep or gone by the time I get back tomorrow. But I really am so fond of it and delighted that I didn't want to wait till the time you came back to tell you. So thank you loads and loads and you really shouldn't have bothered, being so tired and everything, but I can't help being so glad you did. Have a good trip and a good rest,[3] and I'll see you when you come back. And a Merry Christmas, sleeping or waking, and a specially happy New Year.

Love Nowell

1. A porcelain figurine of an angel.
2. A reference to her work with LeGette Blythe's biography of the Napoleonic general.
3. Wolfe was planning to spend Christmas with the Aswell family in Pleasantville.

🌷 🌷 🌷   December 29, 1937.

Dear Miss Nowell:

Thanks for your letter.

There is nothing much to report, except that Aswell brought me the contract and I took it up to the Authors' League, which I joined, yesterday afternoon, and I am going back to the Authors' League today. The man at the Authors' League, who reads contracts, objected vigorously in several places, and thought there were several clauses which ought to be changed, and several more which ought to be left out entirely. Since they seem to be on the side of the author, and looking out for his interest, I told him to go ahead and revise the contract the way he thought it ought to be, to take care of my interest, but not to needlessly annoy or offend the publisher, because I thought having their good-will is important and valuable also, and I didn't want to do anything willfully that might impair it. He agreed with this, so we'll see what the result is today. Anyway Aswell knew that I was going to the Authors' League and agreed that it was a good thing to do, so I don't think he will hold it against me if some things have been changed that were in his contract.

And by the way, I guess I was wrong about the fifteen thousand: it reads for ten,[1] but I didn't say anything about it, because I know if he had promised fifteen it would have read that way. I think he may have said that I could get that much if I insisted. Anyway, the man at the Authors' League didn't seem to think it would be an awfully good idea to try to press it: he said that I should think for the future too, and that if I insisted on so big an advance that the publisher might not make it back, or had to scrabble for it, it would not be good on either side,—either as regards future books or future publishing relations. He did seem to think that I might be able to get more than 15%, if I insisted—he said that some of their authors did get more, and he mentioned Kenneth Roberts. But, of course, Kenneth Roberts is a big money maker, his books sell way over a hundred thousand and I suppose he doesn't present the publishing problem that I do. Authors' League admitted that 15% was good and generous, so I suppose I'll let it stand at this.

There were one or two other things in the contract that bothered me in any reference they might have to you: The chief one was a clause naming Harpers as my agent on a 10% basis for moving picture, sound, visual, etc. rights. But the Authors' League man pounced on that one any way and is going to take it out: He said the trouble with it is that it gives Harpers an absolute power of disposition which an ordinary agent would not have, and that if some outside agent did come to me with a good offer for a moving picture, sound, visual etc. rights, I would still have to deal with Harpers. Anyway, I guess that is out, so you and I can talk about it when you come back.

There was another clause about "abridgment and selection rights." As Ed explained it, I believe this refers to the boys at colleges who have a nice little racket of their own of writing the author, and getting his permission to use something of his in an anthology they are getting out for their classes, free for nothing. Harpers wants the right to deal with this also, I believe, on a 10% basis: I don't think it would affect you in any case, because I don't believe you have ever handled it for me, have you?—it is perhaps only something out of a story—but anyway, it's out for the present, so we can jaw about that, too.

In other words, no one is going to take one little red penny of the old gotten gains which have enabled you thus far to wallow in luxury at my expense—no sir, by gum, not if I can help it. I really think Ed tried to do the best he could for me on the contract, but I think also I am doing the right thing by getting the Authors' League boy to look it over and revise it before I sign up.

Ed suggested to me that it would be a good idea for me to get it settled up as quickly as possible before the first of the year, because of the income tax. That is, he suggested that I might get half the advance this week before the year is out, and half next month, or at some later time, so that the tax would be divided in two years. What do you think? The trouble is, I always want to talk to you, and the little problem that is bothering me now is whether it will be cheaper to get it divided, or have it all paid next year. I think practically all of my so-called income this year has passed through your own fair hands—but I believe it amounts to considerable, so I am not sure whether it would be cheaper to tack half the advance on to it now, or let the advance go until next year. On the other hand, it will not hurt my feelings a bit if you succeed in selling the Red Book and the Saturday Evening Post a dozen stories next year, in which case—well, you get the point.

I think on the whole this describes the situation, and if anything does occur to you, I wish you would call me up tomorrow morning (Thursday) just as soon as you get this letter. And I guess this is all for the present—I've got to hike it now to the Authors' League, except to say I know I've been a pain in your neck for the last two or three weeks, but that I think a better day is dawning for us both. Anyway "that is no agent, that is my friend" is the way I really feel. and in one way or another I'll try to live up to it.

We really did have a swell Christmas out at Ed Aswell's—I think it was the best one I have had since I was a kid. There were a lot of nice people and every one was really very happy and very moved, and as we were finishing dinner Mary Lou[2] whispered to me and asked me if it was "all right to tell them," and I said "yes," so we got out your bottle of champagne and Mary Lou filled everyone's glass and we all stood up and Mary Lou told them, and I tried to say something and Ed tried to say something, and neither could very well, and everyone had tears in their eyes, and I think they meant it, too. That's why it is a little tough to have to wrangle about contracts now, but I guess that's life, isn't it? And we were right both times. Anyway, dear Agent, I send you my love and with all my heart my wishes for nothing but the best for both of us next year. This goes for your mother too. Please tell her so.

Call me tomorrow morning, *please*, if anything occurs to you. Meanwhile, with all of the best

Yours, Wolfe

1. In his first discussion with Wolfe, Aswell had made an offer of $10,000 in advance royalties for Wolfe's next book.
2. Mrs. Edward Aswell.

❧   ❧   ❧   The Consolvo Hotels
                                   Richmond, Va.
                                   Sunday Jan 9, 1938

Dear Nowell:

Got your letters and enclosures O.K.—I have just passed a week end out in the country that would make the wildest imaginings of

W. Faulkner sound like Winnie The Pooh—"Great Material"—had no rest for the weary! Now, by Mephistopheles, I am going to get a day or two to myself if I have to start a war to do it! Hope I get back in time to have lunch with Aswell and Priestley.[1] Meanwhile, love and best of luck—don't know where I'll go but probably North—Baltimore or Pennsylvania—its less decayed—

Yours, Wolfe

1. J. B. Priestley, the British novelist and man of letters, who was very interested in Wolfe's work.

                                    January 13, 1938
Dear Wolfe:

Here at last is the money from Vogue:[1] $400 minus $40 to me. I'm sending down copies of the various letters they wrote me to Ed, so that he'll have it on record that all the rights business is clear and as it should be.

Guess this is all for now, but hope you and David[2] are having a good time.

Yours, Nowell

1. For "Prologue to America," which appeared in *Vogue*, February 1, 1938.
2. David Gambrell, Wolfe's nephew, who was traveling with him in the South.

114 East 56th Street
New York
January 18, 1938
Dear Wolfe:

I got your friend Cornelius[1] on the phone and he read me long clauses out of the agreement with Madeleine Boyd. It seems that she is entitled to "10% of all royalties paid on the sales of copies of the book LOOK HOMEWARD, ANGEL published *under now existing contracts secured by her*." But under these contracts only, which Mitchell listed to me: the Scribner's contracts, Modern Library, Bonniers, Steenske, Rowohlt, Heinemann and whatever the name of that Czechoslovakia publisher is. She doesn't get 10% on any further sales under new contracts, so that if we did finally sell the book in France, we would be completely free of her. This is just for your own information, because nobody is getting tied up on anything in this French business as yet, until Mr. Raimbault[2] has read copies of LOOK HOMEWARD, ANGEL and OF TIME AND THE RIVER and given up his reaction.

Mitchell said that he didn't like to push you but he wondered if you had done anything about getting Reuter[3] to testify in the manuscript case. He said he thought that would be very important, so I told him I would pass the word on to you by way of a reminder or something.

Yours, Nowell

1. Cornelius Mitchell of Mitchell and Van Winkle, the law firm that represented Scribner's.

2. R. N. Raimbault, the translator for *Nouvelle revue française* and associated with the French publishing house, Gallimard.

3. Barnet Ruder, who eventually did testify. Wolfe won his case against Dooher and retrieved his manuscripts.

Hotel Chelsea
222 West 23rd
New York, New York
March 9, 1938

Dear Miss Nowell:

I have read Mr. Raimbault's letter of February 28th, about translation and publication of "Look Homeward Angel" and "Of Time and the River," and if you think it advisable you can communicate to him the contents of this letter.

I should certainly much rather see the books brought out in France complete, as they were written, even if that involves some such arrangement as Mr. Raimbault speaks of, than have them brought out in condensed or mutilated form. I think I understand the publishing difficulties of which he speaks, and would be willing to yield to them in order to get the books brought out in their entirety and by a competent translator. His letter seems sincere and honest, and if he is a translator of Faulkner he must also be a person of considerable competence.

About the arrangement that he suggests—of bringing "Look Homeward Angel" out in two volumes and "Of Time and the River" in three—I think, if we agree to it, we ought to also be sure that the division which is made is not only good from the point of view of size and length, but also good from the point of view of substance—that is, so far as we are able, that each of the proposed volumes will have a certain unity in itself. Also, what guarantees can we have that the whole work will be published? I mean, it would be rather futile, from my own point of view, to bring out only one or two of the whole five volumes and let the others lapse, because that would not only give no idea of the whole thing, but would also probably make future publication of the complete work in French impossible. I think you ought to find out about these things and protect us in every way you can.

I agree with Mr. Raimbault that publication of the two books in France would probably constitute something of a publishing risk and would call for a publisher with a good deal of courage and belief. I am willing to take all this into consideration when discussing terms; on the other hand, I do not think it should lead us to make unfair concessions. Why don't you try to find out from Faulkner's agent, or whoever may have dealt for him in this matter, just what his own terms were for "Sanctuary," which Mr. Raimbault says he translated, and which had a literary success in France. It seems to me we would have the right to expect terms as favorable for ourselves. And if the books were to be published in five separate volumes under separate titles, how are the contract or contracts to be made out: do we get a separate advance and a separate royalty on each, or is it to be done under the form of a single agreement, covering the whole work?

I know you have thought about all these things, but with a project that has as many complications as this one could have, I think it would be just as well to make sure at the beginning where we stand and in what ways we are involved. You might even communicate with the American publishers of Jules Romains or Proust—I mention them only because their works have also been brought out piecemeal in this country, and their publishers perhaps might be able to give you some advice or information that might be useful to us.

As to the French agent whose name you mentioned, and with whom you have already had negotiations, I am willing to do whatever you think right and fair by her, if this present transaction goes through. I should not think, however, she would be involved for anything more than the one book for which she dealt.

This is all now. Mr. Raimbault seems genuinely interested, and my impression from his letter is that he is a competent and reliable person. You can carry on now in whatever way seems best to you. Let me know what happens.

Yours, Wolfe

❧ ❧ ❧

Hotel Chelsea
222 West 23rd St.
New York, New York
March 22, 1938

Dear Miss Nowell:

Ed Aswell has written telling me he has had a letter of inquiry concerning my next book from a German publisher named Hyperion

Verlag. They want to know what, if any, are my publishing arrangements in Germany, what the subject matter of the new book will be, whether I have an English publisher, and whether they could get a four to six weeks' option on the book—whatever that may mean.

I wrote Aswell and explained the situation and answered all the questions as best I could—as I think you know the situation anyway I will not repeat it here. Aswell felt that it was perhaps better for Harpers not to be mixed up in any negotiations or correspondence with Hyperion Verlag, so I am writing to ask you if you know or could find out anything about them. At best, anything to do with German publishing at the present time seems to be a long and rather forlorn shot: I do not see any prospect of getting anything out of Rowohlt, after what they have done, but I certainly do not want them to keep on pirating my books even if it is Germany. Again, there is not much point in letting a new publisher bring them out, if there is no chance of getting any money for them. However, if you can find out anything about this Hyperion firm, I might follow it up with a letter to them.

This is all now. Sorry you could not make it Sunday. The Dashiells came and I think we had a good time. With best wishes

Yours, Wolfe

114 East 56th Street
New York
March 23, 1938

Dear Wolfe:

It seems sort of funny that neither I nor a big firm that does so much with foreign rights like Harper's has never heard of Hyperion Verlag. Of course they may be damn good for all we know, and I maybe wouldn't be as apt to know as Harper's because I usually let a regular German agent like Li Wegner do the submitting to the general publishing field in Germany. But off-hand I'd say that probably they are not as tops in the field as, say, Fisher (cher?) Verlag about whom you were thinking some time ago, or E. P. Tal Verlag in Vienna who asked for Time and the River and said that if you were ever free from Rowohlt they'd like to know about it. There we run into the Austrian business which God knows nobody knows about right now, but I spose if I'm going to get political about it I might wonder if there would be a war with Germany by the time your next book came out, which might change conditions even more.

I think the main thing is that your reception in Germany makes you likely to be able to arrange for your next book with almost any topnotch German publisher, and it would be better to pick the one you like best—maybe Fisher—rather than get mixed up with Hyperion just by the accident of their having written you. However, I'll try to mosey around a little bit and see what I can find out about Hyperion, but without asking a German agent for fear they might want to horn in on the business. I'll probably be seeing a lot of other agents at all these literary parties that are going on now, so will ask around among them discreetly, without mentioning anything about you by name. So keep your fingers crossed and I'll see what I can find out.

I got a note from Mary Lou saying how swell it was to have you, and Judy was here with her big blue eyes popping out with admiration of you, who she thinks is a "really great person." I'm sorry as hell I couldn't get there, but maybe I'll manage it next time.

Yours, Nowell

🌷 🌷 🌷   114 East 56th Street
New York
March 27, 1938

Dear Wolfe:

Herewith a copy of a nice letter about No More Rivers from your old pal Miss Helen McAfee of the Yale Review. I think it'll work out fine as long as we got along OK on Chickamauga, because at least in this instance it's not a question of hits and thars but just of cutting a little. So let me know if you agree and I'll write her as soon as I hear from you. Incidentally you'd better give me some idea of when you'd be apt to go to the country, if any, so that we can be sure to get this off our chests before you depart.

No information yet on Hyperion in Germany from other agents that I've seen, but I'll keep asking and maybe get the real inside dope soon.

Yours in haste, Nowell

Wolfe Assembles His New Novel

During 1938 Elizabeth Nowell became the most important person in Wolfe's literary life. Because his publishing relationship with Scribner's had been broken off with some bitterness, he no longer saw his former friends in the editorial office, although he met once with Perkins for an amiable luncheon after winning one of his distressing lawsuits. Miss Nowell's office became his business address and he now consulted her about all his literary and personal problems as he once had laid them before Perkins.

But the biggest problem was one he had to solve alone. He spent the time from March to May organizing his great mass of manuscript, arranging material he had written about Eugene Gant and other autobiographical figures so that it would fit into the story of George Webber.

His problem of how to conclude the book moved toward solution when he was asked to speak at the annual literary banquet at Purdue University. He decided to tell the students how he arrived at his present view of life and to use that statement as the final portion of his book, a point at which George Webber addresses a letter of parting to his editor, Foxhall Edwards.

Because he planned a vacation trip to the West Coast after the Purdue speech, he stored his crates of manuscripts and papers in the Harper warehouse for safekeeping. At the same time, he gave Edward Aswell a huge stack of typescript that comprised the draft of his book, now entitled "The Web and the Rock," and he asked Aswell to read through it while he was away. Later Aswell was to edit this material and, after extensive cutting, publish it as three volumes of fiction, The Web and the Rock *(1939),* You Can't Go Home Again *(1940), and* The Hills Beyond *(1941).*

❦ ❦ ❦   April 1st 1938

Mr. S. A. Cummings[1]
Purdue University
Lafayette, Ind.
Dear Mr. Cummings:

  Thomas Wolfe is out of town at the present time with no definite forwarding address. Therefore Charles Scribner's Sons has referred your telegram to me, since I am his literary agent. I think he will probably be back in New York some time next week and will see to it that he receives your telegram as soon as he arrives. However, because there has already been a few days delay, I wanted to write and explain the situation to you.

Sincerely yours,

Dear Wolfe:

Hope this'll hold em till you get back and also that you are getting some real peace and quiet for once in your life.   EN.

1. Professor of English at Purdue University, who invited Wolfe to be the speaker at the annual literary banquet in May.

Hotel Chelsea
222 West 23rd Street
New York, New York
April 5, 1938

Dear Miss Nowell:

I was out of town almost all of last week, and am just getting back to work again—hence my delay in answering your various letters.

I telegraphed the man at Purdue University and asked him to let me know more specifically what he wanted. If he expects some formal prepared speech, than I am out: I haven't got time for it, and besides I wouldn't be good at it. But if I could go out and simply get up and talk to them informally as I did in Colorado I might do it: it wouldn't call for much preparation, because I could just get up and tell them what is on my mind about writing, and since writing is on my mind all the time, it might be interesting. It would certainly be more interesting than a prepared speech.

I also read the enclosed copy of the letter from the French agent, and note what she has to say about our translator. I am going to leave it to you to decide who and which: I do not know either of the people; I suppose always in matters of this sort there is danger of a little professional back-knifing among the interested experts—you know them better than I do so try to judge matters for yourself.

Please write Miss McAfee and tell her that I will be very glad to have "No More Rivers" published in The Yale Review, and that I shall not only be very glad to have her suggestions about cuts, but that I think I can make some good cuts and some improving revisions of my own when I go back to the piece. I am glad there is no great rush about it because I want to go ahead now on the book as hard as I can for the next two months. But you let me know what she says and when you think we ought to get busy on it, and I will be ready for you.

I was awfully tired, but I feel better now as a result of my vacation. If you hear of any likely places that I might live and work in this summer I wish you would let me know. I think what I would like would be a comfortable barn with a good roof and a floor—that is to say, it does not have to be fancy, but I would like a good room to work in, and furthermore, I would like to have my own place—that is, no boarding houses or country inns. If anything occurs to you please let me know.

This is all for the present. I hope this finds you well and everything O.K. With best wishes,

Yours, Wolfe

❧ ❧ ❧

114 East 56th Street
New York
April 5, 1938

Dear Wolfe:

Guess who just blew in but your old friend Mr. H. Tatnall Brown of Haverford with a whole new set of first editions for you to sign.[1] I explained that you were away, but promised that when you came back I would take them down to you and wait until you signed them and then mail them back registered, insured, and everything with my own fair hands. So I'll keep them safe here in one of my tin boxes until you show up and give me a ring to say that you're back.

Did I tell you that I wrote Miss McAfee of the Yale Review explaining that you were away and assuring her that you'd be delighted to see her suggested cuts in "No More Rivers." So everything is under control and I Do hope you'll be rested when you get this.

Yours, Nowell

1. The first set of books that Brown had sent was lost in the mail.

❧ ❧ ❧

[95 Madison St.
New Bedford, Mass.]
April 28, 1938

Dear Wolfe:

Vogue just forwarded the enclosed postcard to me, and I want to see what you think of it. As far as money (if any) goes, I can find out from the Author's League how much we'd be justified in asking for the City Woman's Club of Louisville's use of it.[1] But what I want to

know is whether the whole thing looks too damn awful to you—
whether you think it's OK to let the City Woman's Club of Louisville
cut and choralize your piece, or whether you suspect, as I do, that
they'd make it something sort of awful somehow. Or am I being too
artistic pure, or maybe does my deep ingrained complex and phobia
of women's clubs make me view this idea with too much alarm?

Well, anyway, think it over and I'll give you a ring on Monday to
see how you feel on the subject. Miss Krainin says you called up but
insisted that there was nothing important. But I'll be back Monday
anyway, and we'll talk everything over then.

> Yrs in haste, out to play
> tennis with my energetic mamma
> Nowell

PS I'm keeping a copy of Miss Madge P. Stoner's postcard so as to
have her address, etc. in case you lose the original.

1. The club members wished to stage a dramatic presentation of "Prologue to
America."

❦   ❦   ❦

> Hotel Chelsea
> 222 West 23rd St.
> New York, New York
> April 29, 1938

Dear Miss Nowell:

I got your letter with the attached postcard from Madge P. Stoner.
Life is very strange. No, I do not think I have any serious twinges of
artistic conscience about letting the Louisville Woman's Club use it,
except I would like to know what they do with it, and what they
propose to cut. I suppose it really would not do us any damage to let
them have it—but we will talk it over when you get back.

I am meeting Aswell this afternoon and going home with him, and
we are starting out on a week-end jaunt tomorrow morning to look
at possible places for the summer. He suggested that we might be
gone Monday, too, and asked me to make allowances for this. I
think we probably will be if they still plan to visit Professor and Mrs.
Saunders.[1] But I will see you when I get back. I would also like to
show you some things and talk to you before I go West around May
19th. But we will have time in the next two weeks.

I hope you are getting a good vacation and come back feeling fit.
With best wishes,

> Yours, Wolfe

1. Dr. A. P. Saunders, professor of chemistry and formerly dean of Hamilton College, Clinton, New York.

[April 1938]
Dear Wolfe:
   I thought you might like to see this, though there's no special rush
about it. I've written her[1] to say thank you and that I'm forwarding
the note to you. I've also told her that I've been scrupulously avoid-
ing you so you'd work on the big job of the book, but that I'm sure
there'll be some fine things for her sooner or later anyway. So we can
let it go at that, or if you have something special you want me to
show her—maybe even in rough draft before we do a lot of work on
it—we could do so. I was thinking of the "Counting from the Left"[2]
piece that I discouraged you so cruelly on, but which we could show
her now to get her reaction if you wanted. I've still got that in my
strong box in the office. Well, don't let it go and get you off the book
if you're going strong on that. But I'll be talking to you on the phone
anyway when I get back the first of the week.
                                    Love, Nowell

   1. Katharine S. White of the *New Yorker*.
   2. The material about "Preacher Reed" which later was incorporated into Chapter
11 of *The Web and the Rock*.

                                    Hotel Chelsea
                                    222 West 23rd Street
                                    New York, New York
                                    May 3, 1938
Dear Miss Nowell:
   I came back last night and got your note with the letter from The
New Yorker. I think you are handling it just right—and we un-
doubtedly will have something sooner or later that we want to send
them—perhaps even good Dr. Turner[1] if I get around to giving him
another go. But there will be many other things as well.
   Anyway, I want to see you very soon now before I go West[2] and
go over the whole business with you: I have only got an even two
weeks from today, and I think it would be a good idea if we could get
together sometime this week—say, Saturday or Sunday. The most
immediate thing of interest I want to talk to you about is this:—I
finally wrote The Nation and rejected the proposal for the *Living
Philosophies* piece,[3] on the ground that it would take too much time,
and would take me away from my work. At the same time I made
another suggestion to them. I told them about the Purdue engagement, and told them that I proposed to go out and talk to the students right out of the workshop, so to speak—to tell them what I
thought and felt about writing, what I think I have learned about it,

what change and development has come about in me, and what convictions and beliefs I now have, not only about writing, but about the life around me from which I draw the sources of my material, and the writer's place in the whole world today.

As you know, this has been the principal thing that has interested me for at least a year now; it is at the bottom of everything that has happened—beginning with The New Republic piece,[4] leading up through all the Scribner trouble to the place where I now am, and the work I am now doing. I believe the time has come when I am ready to say it, and if the time has come and I can say it, it will knock The New Republic piece into a cocked hat because it will shoot the works.

What I did, therefore, first of all, was simply to dictate a very plain and simple account of things to use at the Purdue gathering. Of course, it is immensely too long, and besides towards the end there are many, many things in it of too personal and complex a nature for an occasion of that sort. However, it did serve the purpose of getting certain things on record, and as for the Purdue thing, I do not think I shall have any difficulty with that at all, nor even have to refer to a typed sheet, because I know pretty clearly in my mind now what I am going to say to them, and what will probably be most appropriate for an occasion like that.

The Nation suggested that I show them the Purdue thing pretty much as I gave it to the students, but I do not want to do this, because I think the final outcome may be so much better.[5] Briefly, what I am trying to do, as with everything in which I am most deeply interested, is to give the piece at the end the depth and permanence of imaginative truth. I hope this does not make you smile—for that is the idea.

For months now, it has occurred to me that I would conclude the tremendously long book on which I am working with a kind of epilogue that takes the form of a personal address—to be called "You Can't Go Home Again," or "A Farewell to the Fox," or perhaps by still another title. That epilogue, as I have conceived it, would be a kind of impassioned summing up of the whole book, of everything that has gone before, and a final statement of what is now. The book will certainly close in some such way as this, although it may turn out at the end that the method of personal address, even in high poetic terms, is not the best way to conclude a book in which the whole narrative, hundreds of characters, and the events of more than a hundred years are stated objectively. However that may be, it is not important here, for if I succeed in doing "You Can't Go Home Again," or "A Farewell to the Fox," as I want to do it, it will stand most tremendously on its own legs. Anyway, that is what I am doing now: transforming the material for the simple Purdue statement into the terms of poetic and imaginative fact—into the truth of fiction—because it seems to me that it is really my essential job. What do you think of it?

I have written The Nation and more or less committed myself to letting them see it, but of course, three thousand words is nonsense—thirty thousand probably will be likelier, if I can hold it down to that—they realize, although I have not explained to them what it is as I have to you—that the thing is probably out of the question for them—unless they want to pull a big one, and match their distinguished rival of a year ago. This, of course, in case it is good—sooner or later, it will be good, it must be, because it is so deep in me—but I hope it is good now. I have only two weeks more to work on it—and if I was fresh, I believe I could almost put it through, because usually the length of time a piece of writing takes—the best writing, that is—can never be reckoned except in terms of the days and months and years it has been coming to a head. That certainly has happened with this one—and I know that I am ready; but it may be I have to take another breather before I put it through. I suppose I may take the Purdue trip as the chance to get one—the chance to get away by myself on a streamlined train for a week or two—before I come back and settle in for the summer.

I had a nice trip with the Aswells, and saw some beautiful country, and one or two places which are possibilities for the summer, all of which I shall tell you about when I see you. Think over what I said to you and let me know. Also call me up and tell me what is a convenient date for our get-together—almost any time you mention will do for me.

This is all now, and I hope this finds you well. With best wishes,

Sincerely, Wolfe

1. "Portrait of a Literary Critic," a satirical treatment of Henry Seidel Canby, which was published in the *American Mercury*, April 1939, and later included in *The Hills Beyond*.

2. Wolfe planned to take a vacation trip to the West Coast after his speaking engagement at Purdue.

3. Freda Kirchwey, editor of *The Nation*, had asked Wolfe to contribute an essay on his philosophy of life to a series of articles entitled *Living Philosophies* that were later to be collected and published as a book by Simon and Schuster.

4. "I Have a Thing to Tell You."

5. Wolfe did prepare a typewritten copy of his speech; it was published as *Thomas Wolfe's Purdue Speech "Writing and Living,"* edited by William Braswell and Leslie A. Field, (West Lafayette, Ind.: Purdue University Press, 1964). In revised form, this material became the concluding chapters of *You Can't Go Home Again*.

❦ ❦ ❦   114 East 56th Street
                                         New York
                                         May 11, 1938

Dear Mr. Wolfe:

It looks as if this was going to be fanmail.[1] But ever since I was there Monday night I've been thinking how swell the first big hunk— and all the other later hunks—of the book are. I too am "honored to have read it," and, too, in the real sense of the words.

So many reviewers have yapped so much about the "great American novel" and in connection with so many piddling writers that it sounds almost silly to use the phrase now. But again going back to the "real sense of the words," I think you're it, Toots. Because nobody else in the world could get the real flavor of those tough, salty, swell old guys like Bear and Zach and the way they talked and thought and lived so perfectly, with all the juice still there as if this was still the early rough and ready frontier America. And what's more, nobody in the world but you could bring that to life and then keep all your juice and understanding right in stride and perfect tune with the whole of changing history and come through to the swell and right-in-the-present-and-future stuff like the last parts of the book: the whole New York modern life, the literary racket, the German Nazi stuff, the ruined town and the Parson and police, and —well, the whole analysis of the world right this minute.

God knows if this sounds too grandiloquent because I've got some sweeping phrases in what I've just ripped off above without premeditation. But honestly, they really fit here and they aren't grandiloquent because it's the truth, so help me God. So well, there's no special reason in writing this except to say what I've been so full of ever since Monday. And also maybe to remind you when you're tired and sort of appalled by the work still before you, that nobody can get the whole of the U.S. on the head of a pin. It's a great book and nobody but you in the whole wide world could do it, and the more I think and see of it the more steamed up I am.

                                         Love, Nowell

1. As he was assembling his huge manuscript for the novel that he called "The Web and the Rock," Wolfe let Nowell read through the first portion of it about the Joyners, which she had not seen before.

Hotel Chelsea
222 West 23rd Street
New York, New York
May 12, 1938

Dear Miss Nowell:

Both Miss Jassinoff[1] and I were glad to hear from you, and to know that there is a prospect of your having work for her to do. I would be delighted, of course, if it could work out this way: it is mighty nice of you to suggest it, and if it does turn out that you have work to give her, I know you would have no reason to regret it.

I don't suppose I will see you again before I go away, but I'll get in touch with you just as soon as I get back. I don't know where I'm going after I get through at Purdue—a little fellow named Joe Brewer (do you remember him? He used to be Brewer and Warren) is now, believe it or not, president of Olivet College, in Olivet, Michigan, and wants me to come there and talk to them, after Purdue. But I think this is out, because if I'm going to get any rest at all, I think this is my chance.

I will be gone two or three weeks, and I am going West somewhere from Purdue—but I'll write or wire you and let you know. I'll be back here by the early part of June and if I go out of town, I'll get together with you on the Yale Review piece[2] and anything else that may come up before I do leave town.

It was awfully good of you to write me as you did. Naturally, it makes me feel good, and somehow, although I am appalled at the job I have cut out for myself, I think it is going to be all right. I am tired, but otherwise I have not felt such hope and confidence in many years. It may be that I have come through a kind of transition period in my life—I believe this is the truth—and have now, after a lot of blood-sweat and anguish, found a kind of belief and hope and faith I never had before.

At any rate, I am going to try to put it all into the book, and if you stand by and put in an occasional comforting word to people who may be getting restive—that would be swell. I am sorry that you didn't see more of it the other night—but nowadays I am a little too fagged to do the whole thing at once. There has not been much let-up since I went to Germany two years ago—and there wasn't much then, because I found out I couldn't go back to Europe again as if I were taking a trip on a Coney Island pleasure boat: anyway, it's all gone into the mill, and I hope it comes out the right way.

This is packing up day—I approach with considerable fear and trembling the job of assembling a good part of the manuscript I have done in the last three or four years. We are trying to arrange and audit it, so to speak, in some convenient form.

Aswell is going to keep it for me until I get back, but I don't know whether it would be a good idea to let him read it now or not. I know where I stand, but it is like presenting someone with the bones of some great prehistoric animal he has never seen before—he might be bewildered. Anyway, I will know in a few days when I get it together. I have an idea I've got something roughly similar—so far as state of completion is concerned—to the first rough draft of OF TIME AND THE RIVER—which Perkins saw at the end of December, 1933. I hope this is true, but even if it is, I am not certain whether it would be a good thing for Ed to read it now. I have written and explained the situation to him, and I think he understands it. I have a very strong hunch that I know where I am going a lot more clearly that I ever did before, and for that reason, I am not sure that it would be the best thing to have editorial advice and revision at this present time.

I hope also, that he is able or will consent to take care of the rest of my stuff at Harper's until I get back. This business of being a vagabond writer with two tons of manuscript is not an easy one, particularly when one is going off somewhere, and does not want and cannot afford to keep on paying rent for an establishment he is no longer using. I had a letter from an autograph and manuscript dealer this morning, and I suppose he would gladly volunteer to keep it *but—*

This is all now. I will call you up if I have time before I leave on Tuesday night. If not, I'll see you when I return. And I hope it does turn out you can get together with Miss Jassinoff.

Meanwhile, good luck and all good wishes,

Sincerely, Wolfe

1. Gwen Jassinoff, Wolfe's typist during the recent months.
2. "No More Rivers."

*Wolfe's talk at Purdue was an enormous success. Then his trip to
Washington and Oregon extended into a two-week tour of eleven
national parks in the company of two newspapermen who were
preparing a travel article. Soon after this exhausting experience, he
caught a cold, which a few days later turned to pneumonia. Friends
in Seattle called in Dr. E. C. Ruge, who placed Wolfe in his private
hospital for treatment, but even though Wolfe recovered from pneumonia, he continued to have intermittent fever. For consultation,
Dr. Ruge called in Dr. Charles Watts, who moved Wolfe to a hospital
in Seattle for x-ray tests. The results showed a spot on Wolfe's right
lung, a condition that the doctors could not agree about in their
diagnoses.*

*The letters that close this book extended over the summer of 1938
during which time Elizabeth Nowell tried in her cheery way to offer
Wolfe her best encouragement for recovery.*

🌢 🌢 🌢   Auditorium Hotel
Chicago
Monday May 23, 1938

P.S. Dear Nowell: Please send enclosed letter of recommendation to
Miss Jassinoff *right away*!

Dear Miss Nowell:

Thanks for sending the telegram to Purdue: I don't know who
Miss Cabot is or what the houseparty is about—it sounds a little Ox-
ford-Movementy, doesn't it? Everything went off beautifully at Purdue—I talked and I talked, there was great applause, and everyone
seemed satisfied:—also I met some very nice young people—teachers
and instructors and their wives who took care of me—we all drove
up to Chicago together Friday night,[1] and we spent two very pleasant days together, eating, drinking, driving all over Chicago, visiting
the *stupendous* University—exploring the magnificent Lake Front—
and the not so magnificent slums—I really got it to a T in the Vogue
piece—all of the grandeur and the misery of America is here—and
yesterday we spent the whole day at the Brookfield Zoo—which is
superb! I fed packages of crackerjacks to the polar bears who wave

their paws at you coyly and beat anything for charm you ever saw—
my friends left last night—and I am on my way West this afternoon
—don't quite know where yet—but probably to Colorado, first by
one of the streamlined Zephyrs (it's only overnight this way—1100
miles across the continent and the plains in 15 hours—how's that?)
and later perhaps to the North West—I hope nothing comes up that
I have to be bothered about—everything's going to be O.K. now if I
get a little uninterrupted rest—the Middle-Western thing—India-
napolis, Purdue, and all of it—was swell!—People say you'd get
tired of it—but it was fat as a hog and so fertile you felt that if you
stuck a fork in the earth the juice would spurt—one thousand miles
of fat, flat, green, hog-fat fertility—barns, houses, silos, towns—the
whole repeating in the recessions of a giant scroll—very restful somehow, after the torment of N.Y. and four million words of mss. (Aswell got the mss before I left—I finished completely and was completely finished!—He wanted very much to read it—I had misgivings
but he swore I could trust him to understand the unfinished state of
things and to feel what I am about—and I hope to God he does, and
that it is all right for him to read it now—it would be a crime if I
were interrupted or discouraged now!)

    Good-bye for the present, and try to take care of anything that
comes up—I'll let you know where I am—

                         With best wishes, yours,
                              Wolfe
P.S. I'm staying here in an old hotel—not unlike the Chelsea—which
I've always wanted to stay at because we had a book when I was a
child called Wonders of Science or The Marvels of the Modern Age
—with a picture of the hotel—have a great big room overlooking the
Lake Front with the whole great system of parks, esplanades, drives,
museums, and freight trains right before me—weather has been in
and out—mostly good—but today awful—trickle of rain and fog
from the lake—hope it clears before I go West.

    1. For an account of Wolfe's stay at Purdue and in Chicago, see Appendix II of
Thomas Wolfe's Purdue Speech "Writing and Living."

                              The Brown Palace Hotel
                              Denver
                              Thursday, May 26, 1938
Dear Miss Nowell:—Got here yesterday after an all night ride at 80
milers per hour across the continent in the Burlington Zephyr—No
sleep, but couldn't quiet down at this altitude of one even mile—
looked up my Denver friends, they gave a swell party for me last

night, and I'm afraid I talked and ate and drank them all into a state of exhaustion—Both newspapers were on my tail 30 minutes after I hit town, and I am sending you a sample of their arts—I'm heading Northwest from here towards Oregon—May miss the Yellowstone because I understand it doesn't open until June 20th—Can't give you any forwarding address, because I don't know any myself at present—Am driving over to Boulder tomorrow to see my friends there—and am leaving here, I think, day after tomorrow (Saturday) —Sending this airmail to you—If anything important turns up, wire me here. Meanwhile, good luck and best wishes.

Wolfe

P.S. One of the people at the party last night was at Bryn Mawr and knows you and [the] Sanders girls—Her married name is Ann Downs (her husband owns big clothing store here)—forget her single one: she is blonde-reddish-and (like so many of the other society ladies here) she sculpts—maybe you can dope out who she is.

114 East 56th Street
New York
May 27, 1938.

Dear Wolfe:

Don't let this frighten you because nothing at all important has happened. I just thought I might as well write in case it reached you, to reassure you that nothing had. There's a whole flock of stuff here, but none of it important, although I may as well tell you what it is in case you are interested.

The only one I'm a little bit doubtful about is your friend Alfred H. Iseley, who wrote you saying he wanted to treasure first editions of your work and wondered if you could find some for him, tell him how much they were so he could pay you and then write something in the front of each. I figured it would be easier for me to take care of it while you were away so you wouldn't be bothered. So I wrote him and got a check and am getting "Time and the River" first from Ruder and have got "Death to Morning" and "Story of A Novel" from Scribner's. Will hold them all here till you get back and I hope to God he isn't somebody that you hate his guts and would rather die than write anything in the front, although in that case, you could just say—To Alfred, from Thomas Wolfe, or some such.

You got a long pleading letter from somebody from Rowohlt—signature very scrawly, flourishy, so I can't read it. As usual, they are begging you to sign your contracts and promising to transfer the money due you on the "Angel" and the "River" saying that they can't transfer the money due on the other two unless you sign the contracts. Well, you know the sort of letter it is and I am leaving it strictly unanswered because I think that is the way you want to treat them—or in any case I won't put my foot in it because it is so delicate a situation.

Also, pleading letters from your friend Mr. Cane[1] and the grocery down in Carolina; bill from Remington, etc., but I guess they all can wait OK. Also a letter from the German lawyer Mr. Westrick, saying that as he has not heard further from you, he thinks your relations with Rowohlt must be satisfactory now (??!!!). He therefore is proposing a fee for his work of $100 (!!).

I've talked to Ed [Aswell] several times on the phone and was going to have lunch with him, but this week was the one in which he had those big sales meetings every single day, so we had to put it off till later. He sounds very devoted to you and said for me to tell you that everything was there safe at Harper's. It was about a week ago that I talked to him and he hadn't read it yet. But I dropped a seed to the effect that I hoped nobody in the Business Department, for instance, would fail to appreciate the book and how it had to be long, and I guess he got the idea, although all he said was no one like that would be allowed to have anything to do with it, etc. I think maybe he will have a lot read by the time I see him and then I can pump him a little more. He was worried about your flying because of all those plane accidents lately and jokingly I said perhaps we should have insured your life for $10,000 and very earnestly and seriously, devotedly, he said that $10,000 was nothing compared to your real worth as the greatest writer he knew, or words to that effect. In other words, don't worry, because I really think the whole thing is going to be OK.

Miss Jassinoff has been here and is a very swell girl—very funny when she tells of her interviews seeking jobs. So far, she hasn't found anything, chiefly because she doesn't know enough shorthand, but I got one story that needed typing and hope that drop in the bucket will help her a little bit. She brought me carbons of the whole outline of the book[2] to keep for you and even though I don't know what some of the sections are, it certainly sounds swell, and certainly as if you had the whole pattern worked out one hundred times better than I ever would have dreamed you had so soon. She likewise thinks you are the most wonderful guy she ever saw—not only as a writer, but a person. She kept saying that even in all that strain of tremendous creative work, you never for one minute were impatient or inconsiderate of her and she had never seen anybody like it in her life.

Ed did what he could for her at Harper's and I wrote her a letter of recommendation and gave her yours. There are a couple of things she wondered if you would mind changing a little speck in yours, although she does want me to thank you a million times for being so thoughtful in getting it typed and to her, in spite of shooting across the continent the way you are. What she wants is pretty harmless, but I'll tell you each phrase so you can see what you think. Instead of saying she worked for you from January to May, she wonders if you would be willing to make it sound vaguer—just say during the past year, in case some prospective employer should say that wasn't enough experience. She also wonders if you could stick something in saying why she is no longer with you, i.e., that you have left New York, so that nobody could think you fired her because of any faults.

[The rest of the letter is missing.]

1. Wolfe was disputing the amount of Melville Cane's bill of $125 for the drawing up of Wolfe's will.

2. See "Thomas Wolfe's Rough Outline of His Last Book" printed as an appendix to Richard S. Kennedy, *The Window of Memory: The Literary Career of Thomas Wolfe* (Chapel Hill: University of North Carolina Press, 1962). Note how the information in this letter destroys the argument of Patrick Miehe, "The Outline of Thomas Wolfe's Last Book," *Harvard Library Bulletin*, October 1973, that Edward Aswell had composed the outline.

The Brown Palace Hotel
Denver
May 31, 1938

Miss Elizabeth Nowell
114 East 56th Street
New York
Dear Miss Nowell:

Thanks for your letter and for all the news. I am returning with this letter a revised copy of the recommendation for Miss Jassinoff, with the corrections as you suggested; and I hope she finds it satisfactory.

I am still here, as you see, and shall probably be here a day or two longer and will then go to Colorado Springs for a day or two to see some friends there. After that, I shall probably take up my deferred trip to the Northwest—probably to Oregon. Anyway, I will let you know. I told everyone here I was staying for just a day but I have been here almost a week already. Everyone has been grand and, although we have practically done away with sleep as a disposable luxury, I am beginning to feel all ironed out again, and I think I will be in pretty good shape to continue the struggle when I get back.

If you have any mail or messages that look interesting or impor-

tant I think you may send them on Air Mail to this hotel. If I have
gone to Colorado Springs, they can forward them on to me. This is
all for now. My fingers have begun to itch already for the pencil, but
I think I will keep away from it if I can for another week or so.

> With all good wishes,
> Yours, Wolfe

❧   ❧   ❧   114 East 56th Street
                                       New York
                                       June 6, 1938

Dear Wolfe:

I didn't answer your first because there wasn't a single thing to tell
you, but now I guess perhaps you were worrying that you didn't
hear from me. There's still absolutely nothing of importance. You
got the usual bills on the first of the month and I note that your
friend Mr. Cane has gone back up to $125, but am not doing any-
thing about it. I guess you will have to wrastle with him somehow
when you get back, but that of course is N.O.M.B.[1] You also got a
bill from Lum, Tamblyn and Fairlie, but it all seems to have been
paid except for a balance of $50. I can't make out if they ever col-
lected costs from Dooher or not, but will just drop them a line saying
that you are away and will leave it for you to settle on your return.

Gave your letter to Miss Jassinoff and she is delighted with same. I
don't think she's got a job yet, but Nancy Hale, thank God, has
started writing stories, so I have a little typing for Miss J. to do at
any rate. You got two postcards, very cute, from David and I sent
him one from New Bedford and got back a humdinger from him, all
of which will keep until you get here, though if you should want to
send him anything very handsome from the great Northwest, I guess
he would love it.

You also got a complementary copy of Nicholas Murray Butler's
address delivered at the commencement of Columbia, entitled "Abdi-
cation of Democracy" which I will save for your delectation on your
return. Otherwise, practically nothing at all, so don't you worry. No
sign of "No More Rivers" from Miss McAfee yet, though perhaps I
shouldn't mention that for fear it will descend from the blue tomorrow or the next day.

Anyway, you go ahead and have a good time. It all sounds swell
and your western journey is bound to turn into something elegant for
the book or magazine or almost anything you say. Guess this is all
for now, though I'm hoping to have lunch with Ed some time this
week and if there's anything worth telling, I'll write you further

afterward. Although again I don't think there's anything in the least to worry about which seems to be my whole refrain for this somewhat piecemeal letter.

Lots of love, in any case

Nowell

1. None of my business.

      Hotel Boise
Boise, Idaho
Monday June 7, 1938

You've no *idea* about the size of the damned thing—and yet it doesn't frighten me!

Dear Nowell:

Just a line to tell you I'll be in Portland tomorrow night—stopped off here today in order to see country tomorrow by daylight—Tomorrow should be wonderful because I get the Columbia river and Oregon—but today:—Idaho. What I saw of it today—is the abomination of desolation—an enormous desert bounded by infinity—faraway mountains that you never get to—and little pitiful blistered towns huddled down in the most abject loneliness underneath the huge light and scale and weather and the astonishing brightness and dimension of everything—all given a kind of tremendousness and terror and mystery by the dimension—and this? Their pride and joy, I guess, set in a cup of utterly naked hills—a clean little town, but with a sparseness—a lack of the color, open-ness, richness of Cheyenne—I've tried to find Fisher[1]—people know him here but he's not in the telephone book—anyway, what I've seen today explains a lot about him—

Best wishes—Wolfe

1. Vardis Fisher's home was in Boise.

University Club
Portland, Oregon
Wed. June 15, 1938

Dear Miss Nowell:

I'm on my way to Seattle in a few minutes after a most wonderful week here—I'll be back here Saturday but am leaving again Sunday morning on what promises to be one of the most remarkable trips of my life. It means I'll be away about two weeks longer than I intended—but it is the chance of a lifetime and after long battlings

with my conscience I have decided I'd be foolish not to take it—
Here's the program: A young fellow I knew on one of the local
papers is starting out Sunday morning in his car on a tour of the
entire West, and he has asked me to come with him—We leave here
Sunday and head South for California stopping at Crater Lake on the
way down—We go down the whole length of California taking in
Yosemite, the Sequoias and any other nat'l. parks they have—Then
we swing east across the desert into Arizona to the Grand Canyon
etc, north through Utah, Zion and Bryce Canyons, Salt Lake etc,
then to Yellowstone, then north to the Canadian Border, Montana,
Glacier Park, etc, then west again across Montana, Idaho, Washington—The Rainier Park—etc—in other words a complete swing
around the West from the Rocky Mtns on, and every big nat'l park in
the West—the cost will be very little as we are stopping at roadside
cabins, etc—he's writing a series of articles to show the little fellow
how inexpensively he can see the West.

The whole thing will take two weeks to the day—perhaps a day
or two less for me, because I intend to leave him at Spokane, and
head straight for N.Y.—I've seen wonderful things and met every
kind of person—doctors, lawyers, lumberjacks, etc—and when I get
through with this I'll have a whole wad of glorious material—My
conscience hurts me about this extra two weeks, but I believe I'd
always regret it if I passed it up—when I get through I shall nearly
have seen America (except Texas)—Why didn't you write? I'm worried. I'll be here at the University Club for a day Saturday—and if
you want to reach me, use this address—Wish I could tell you more
about this wonderful country, but that will come later—Meanwhile,
best wishes—

                                    Wolfe

�', 🌷 🌷   114 East 56th Street
                          New York
                          June 17, 1938.
Dear Don Thomaso:

I *did* write you but neither Miss Krainin nor I could make out the
name of that Portland hotel very well, so maybe it never got there.
Anyway, here's the carbon of it for you now. Since then not much
has happened, though everything OK. Maney and Buckner[1] are raising a little hell about $9.17 they say they've been trying to collect
since last August and are threatening in a feeble way to send a
collector after you. I've written saying that you're still away—that

I'll call the matter to your attention as soon as you return etc. etc. And I guess any bill collector would have a hard time catching up with you at your present rate of travel. Mammoth Storage Warehouse also sent a bill though with no threats attached. Besides Miss Jassinoff says you paid that up to May anyway, so I needn't worry.

More postcards from David, invitation to dinner from one Miss or Mrs. Siler (I wrote her and explained), Robert Miner of Hartford is anxious to get in touch with you, and Mrs. HT Mason was here for a few days from Asheville but I explained to all of them.

So much for your social life, and now for your literary. I had lunch with Ed a few days after writing you last and everything is fine. When he walked in I almost lost my breath because he looked so badly—sort of transparent blue-white and 15 pounds thinner and while I was finishing a phone call he sat on the sofa with that kind of immobility that only old men or invalids or completely exhausted people have. Well, lest this scare you, he now says he's much better. He'd been going through 10 days of "sales conferences" which are always hell on any intelligent editor and doing all his regular work at night. Anyway, he came down with a bad cold the day after I saw him so had to get some rest and is now far better though still coughing a speck on the phone. He was worried sick lest you might get back before he'd finished reading, or lest you might be worrying about it and I said that you wouldn't be back for ages so just to get healthy and not drive himself to read the whole thing against a deadline. So to-day when I got your letter I called up to tell him you'd be gone on a two weeks trip, figuring that would ease his worries a speck. He says that everything is swell, and that when he finishes he'll want to write you or wire you if I have an address then. I said I'd write and tell you that he still hadn't finished but that "everything was fine so far" and he said "NO. Don't say 'so far'—that sounds as if I was reading it with reservations or as if I was suspecting something was going to be wrong and that's exactly the way I'm *not* reading it." In other words—and I'm sorry I didn't take down his exact words in pencil as he said them—he said that he was reading it in an excited maybe even carried-away state of mind, though I don't think Ed used as girlish a word as "carried away" but some other. So anyway, you get the idea, and he will either wire or write or tell you face-to-face in his own words, depending on how soon he gets finished, whether we have any address for you, etc.

Dearie, if you *can*, give me more time to answer your letters. Because this one of yours didn't come until this morning—Friday— and I'm damned if I know whether it'll catch you before you leave or not. Guess you maybe won't have any address while on the motor trip, but I do think it sounds very very swell and very very valuable to you as a writer. And Ed said the same thing.

Miss McAfee says the proofs will be coming next week probably but if they do I'll write and explain that you're still away and get her to postpone it to, say, the winter issue or something of the sort. So go ahead and get all the swell stuff on the country that you want because it's not only good for you physically but as a writer.

Vardis was out in the wilderness of Idaho when you were in Boise but if you should come back through there you can get him at the WPA office, 302 Sonna Building. He's doing a VERY swell book and I'm so excited I can hardly keep it to myself.[2]

I had lunch with Mr. Perkins too and it is sort of tragic and yet it makes me mad as well as miserable to see what a Tory he's turning out to be as he gets old. He began by asking me about you—I think he was trying to find out in his "fox" way if there was going to be anything about Scribner's in your book. So I said I'd read the first big hunk you'd written and that there was NO one in it who could be you or Joe Doaks or any member of the Gant or Doaks families. He said well, didn't I think you'd get back to Doaks later? And I said I didn't know. I guess that was a lie all right but I figured it was none of my business, though again if I'd said "I refuse to answer without advice of counsel" he would have taken it to mean that there was stuff about Scribner's and I was being cagey to prevent him from knowing. Well, I think some of his asking about you—maybe a great part—was because of his real affection and interest in you and your career. But he's so clever that you never can tell. Mme. Sally Saunders suddenly popped up from another booth in a very unbecoming hat and said "Hel-LO!" the way she does. But she didn't come and speak to us or ask about you or anything, just shouted as she went past. So then I got Perkins off you and onto a violent political argument with his ending up more reactionary than anybody in the world and me shouting flaming radical slogans at him, almost. Well, you know how it is when people get in discussions like that with him.[3]

I guess all this will kind of sicken you, way out there with a lot of richness and open air and everything. I mean to hear that the same old music is still going round and round in the NY literary world. But anyway, you just forget it and get a good rest and keep on seeing America and you'll be so many miles above it and beyond it and greater than it that it'll only be like a mosquito humming past.

So now no more if I'm going to have even a prayer of getting this to you in time. But good luck anyway and don't worry about a thing.

Love, Nowell

1. The North Carolina grocers whose bill was still unpaid.

2. *Children of God*, a historical novel about the Mormon settlement in the West, published in 1939.

3. In later years, Nowell commented on this luncheon meeting in a letter to W. A. Jackson, librarian of Houghton Library, January 4, 1951: "Perkins had seemed terribly old and tired and discouraged and tragic, and I told Tom so in my letter. He was upset by world affairs, particularly by Nazi Germany. Said that the world was in a dreadful state, that he was going to bring up his grandson (s?) to be career diplomats, that that was the only thing left for them to have as a career. That fascism was 'all the fault of these communists'—if it hadn't been for them, the communists, there never would have been fascism. . . . We both loved to argue and went at it with great zest. . . . Anyway, we got to shouting at each other . . . but it was all in fun and I was trying to cheer Perkins up." Wisdom Collection, Houghton Library, bMS Am1883.3 (87).

University Club
Portland, Oregon
Sunday, June 19

Dear Miss Nowell:

I got back here from Seattle last night and was delighted to find your letter. Our trip has been postponed until tomorrow morning—the little girl of one of the men was sick, but she's O.K. now, and by cutting a few corners we'll be back on schedule in a day or two. It ought to be a grand trip.

Washington and Seattle were wonderful—and I discovered all of my Westall kin—the progeny of old Bacchus who came out here in the 90s. There are 37 of them now—I have the whole family tree and talked to 3 of them and have the record—I'd like to go back again and get the whole story. To me, it's mighty interesting.

This part of the country is almost fabulous. The streams and creeks and rivers swarm with fish—not 6 inch 12 ounce ones—but great salmon, steelheads, etc that weigh from 10 to 30 pounds. The forests are dense with enormous fir trees four and six feet through—the lumberjacks cut them down, the great lumber mills—I visited one of them—tear and slash and plane them into boards—and the enormous forests keep producing them—they keep growing everlastingly in spite of everything. The people are wonderfully good and open—I think a little too simple, maybe, and uncomplicated and *away* from the rest of the world—but its a swell place and you're willing to believe that almost anything can happen here.

I was glad to get your letter and to know you'd seen Ed Aswell. I'll see him when I get back. I'm looking forward to the trip as a great thing in every way and shall try to put work out of my head till I get back.

I'm sorry about M.P.[1] Everything you tell me about him touches and grieves and hurts me like hell. Please—*please* don't tell him about me, or anything about me, if you can avoid it: for six years he was my friend—I thought the best one I ever had—and then, a little over two years ago he turned against me—everything I have done since was bad, he had no good word for it or for me, it's about as if he were praying for my failure. I can't understand it or fathom it, but it is a sad strange thing. Max still tells people that he is my friend, and then he runs me down; and out here in the West I have run on one or two stories that the Scribners (salesmen) apparently have been instructed to pass around that sicken me.[2] It's like a nightmare, but I won't let it get me down. What is this thing in life anyway that causes people to do things like this? The hell of it is, the people who say they love you are often the ones who do the most to injure you. Mrs. B. has been going around for years bleating about her great love for me, but she has also tried to do everything she can against me, and she has not scrupled to write and speak lies, to spread slander, gossip, and do any dirty thing she could. I can't make it out, and now Perkins, under this mask of friendship, is doing the same thing. I don't think I'll ever change in the way I feel about him—the funny thing is I'm always supposed to be the one who changes, but at the bottom I'm the most solid of the lot. I don't think he *consciously* wants me to fail or come to grief, but it's almost as if *unconsciously*, by doing some kind of *wishful* desire, he wants me to come to grief, as a kind of sop to his pride and his unyielding conviction that he is right in everything—the tragic flaw in his character that keeps him from understanding that he has wronged anybody or made a mistake. That is really his great weakness, and I believe it is at the root of his failure—his growing reaction, his sense of defeat, his personal tragedy in his own life and in his family life that has been so marked in recent years. I shall always remember him as one of the most wonderful people I ever knew—but I have neither time nor energy to cope with this thing in him now: all that I know is that it is against me, and against my work, and I can't give it any sort of break—as much as I can, I want to sever the connection entirely—some day, perhaps, if he is willing, I'll take it up again—but meanwhile, let's not play with fire. Tell him nothing about me or what I'm doing: that's the only way, believe me, to avoid trouble. Anyway, it's not a matter of personalities any more: if I'm wrong it will show in my work: if he's wrong it's going to show in his life.

I'm sorry to keep piling it up, but lay off S.S.[3] too—or rather lay off me when you are with her. I'm afraid she's poison—I've heard the story out here, and I think I've got the answer now—it's probably not deliberate poison, but a kind of Kansas City Rappaccini's Daughter, who can't help what she does. Apparently she's always been a kind of dis-oriented screw-ball, with no center and no base—whirling about here and there—a Fascist today, a Communist tomorrow—alas, alas, a K.C. Junior Leaguer (which is to say a Fascist) all the time.—at any rate, hands off: if I get burnt after this, its my own fault.

To end on a more cheerful note—I know a lot of swell people, and I think you are one of them, and I am proud to know you are my friend. I won't be back to Portland, and since from now on I'll be traveling all the time, I don't know at present what to tell you about mail or how to reach me. Anyway, I'll write you later, and I hope to see you in about 3 weeks.

Yours—Wolfe

1. Maxwell Perkins.
2. When Perkins read this letter at the time Nowell sold her Wolfe letters to William Wisdom, he wrote to her, August 7, 1945: "Were you capable of believing—I know Tom could believe anything when his imagination got working—that we would instruct our salesmen to damage him? Besides, we should betray our profession, and everything we believe in, if we tried to injure a great talent. It's incredible that even Tom could believe that." Wisdom Collection, Houghton Library, bMs Am1883.3 (98).
3. Sally Saunders.

Postcard
View of Crater Lake National
Park, Oregon
Monday, June 20, 1938

We're off—stop # 1, and no post card can ever do justice to the color and magnificence—7500 feet up, and ten feet of snow but on to California tonight.

[unsigned]

Postcard
View of Yosemite National Park,
the three mountain peaks called
The Three Brothers. "This group
the Indians likened to squatting
frogs. Their resemblance depends
on the point of view."
[postmark June 22, 1938]

The one on the left is Canby, the middle one De Voto,[1] with Whitney Darrow on the right. (I'm getting a swell story out of this.)

[unsigned]

1. Bernard De Voto, who had earned Wolfe's enmity when he wrote a critical attack on Wolfe, "Genius Is Not Enough," for the *Saturday Review of Literature*, April 25, 1936. Wolfe's resentment carried over to Canby, who as editor of the magazine had been responsible for publishing it.

                                        Hotel Baxter
                                        Bozeman, Montana
                                        Wednesday Morning
                                        [June 29, 1938]

Dear Miss Nowell:

We're on the last leg of our trip—we've gone over 3300 miles in 8 days and "seen" 9 national parks—We'll do 4500 in all and two more parks by the time I leave my two companions Friday night at Rainier and head in to Seattle. It has been furious, hectic, crowded, and wildly comical—but I've seen a whole lot of the country, and a lot of people and things—Furthermore I've got it all down—in a huge notebook—the whole thing smacked down with the blinding speed and variety of the trip. I'm going into Seattle to sleep a day or two—and perhaps to get the whole thing more or less in its present form (the whole trip from the beginning a week ago, I mean) typed down. Also, I've got to get some sleep before I start East. I'm ready and able to sleep now, but no time for it.

Am sending this to you air mail and want you to write or wire me Hotel New Washington, Seattle, to let me know if everything is O.K. and if its all right to stay a little longer to get the whole thing written and typed up. This is all now—we're on our way today to Glacier Park 400 miles away on the Canadian border—it's 6:45 A.M. and I can't dawdle, dearie, any longer.

                                        Yours—Wolfe

                                        New Washington Hotel
                                        Seattle
                                        Sunday July 3 [1938]

Dear Miss Nowell:

I got here late yesterday afternoon and found telegrams from you and Ed and your air mail was delivered this morning: all of which relieves me and boosts me up no end.—The trip was wonderful and terrific—in the last two weeks I have travelled 5000 miles, gone the whole length of the coast from Seattle almost to the Mexican border, inland a thousand miles and northward to the Canadian border. The national parks, of course, are stupendous, but what was to me far more valuable were the towns, the things, the people I saw—the whole West and all its history unrolling at kaleidoscopic speed. I have written it all down in just this way—with great speed, because I had to do most of it at night before going to bed, usually when we had driven 400 or 500 miles and I was ready to drop with sleep— I've filled a big fat notebook with 30000 words of it, and looking some of it over, it occurs to me that in this way I may have got the whole thing—the whole impression—its speed, variety, etc—pretty well. At any rate I've got a pretty clear record of the whole thing since I left New York 6 weeks or so ago—and after two or three days rest out on Puget Sound somewhere (This is a country fit for Gods— you've never seen anything like it for scale and magnificence and abundance—the trees are as tall as the flatiron building and yet so much in scale that you simply cannot believe until you measure them they are as big—and you throw a hook into some ordinary looking creek and pull out a twelve pound salmon—I assure you these things are literally true—you feel there's no limit, no end to anything—the East seems small and starved and meagre by comparison—and yet I'm glad there is the East, too—we've got to have the East, there's something in the East they don't have here)—Anyway, I'd like to loaf and rest for a few days, and then get it typed—revising as much as I can, but not taking too much time, and putting it down from the beginning like a spool unwinding at great speed—Perhaps it's not ready to use yet, or won't be for a year or two, but I'll have it *down* —and you know what that means to me; and I thought I'd call it *A Western Journal*[1]—Anyway, if that's O.K. by you and Ed that's my present idea—I really feel ready to *go* again—I've had no rest but this movement, the sense of life and discovery, the variety has renewed and stimulated me—writing 30000 words under the circumstances of the past 2 weeks was an accomplishment and proved to me that I am getting ready again, because I *wanted* to write them —couldn't keep from it.

Anyway, use this hotel as an address for the present—if I go to Puget Sound I'll leave an address here, and anyway I'll keep you posted. Now get some rest yourself—and thanks for everything!

Yours, Wolfe

P.S. I'm thinking of buying some firecrackers and spending tomorrow in H.M. Canadian town of Victoria, B.C.

1. The most accurate transcription of "A Western Journal" is found in *The Notebooks of Thomas Wolfe*, edited by Richard S. Kennedy and Paschal Reeves (Chapel Hill: University of North Carolina Press, 1970), vol. 2.

114 East 56th Street
New York
July 12, 1938.

Dear Wolfe:

I guess maybe you had better do something about this[1] p.d.q.: Ed doesn't think you have much, if any, manuscript left there, but he says he isn't sure and anyway it would be a shame to lose all that nice old solid furniture, etc. I just called up the gentleman, Mr. Scanlon, to explain that you had been away for two months and I had been unable to reach you with his bills, etc. He said he would hold things up long enough to give me time to try to reach you by airmail letter, but I think you maybe had better settle it anyway, don't you? Especially if you are apt to be without any address while on your way back East, which might be just about the time when they really did start auction proceedings. Well, anyway, I'll leave it up to you, so want to mail this off in a rush so as to be sure and catch you.

Yours, Nowell

1. Because Wolfe had not paid the bill for storing his furniture and other belongings, the Mammoth Storage Company was threatening to sell it all at public auction.

114 East 56th Street
New York
July 13, 1938.

Dear Wolfe:

This is just to say how terribly terribly sorry I am to hear about your getting so sick and so suddenly; and to sort of reassure you that you're not deserted way out there by yourself. Ed and I only heard about it this morning and have been wiring and phoning like mad, and only just now found out what it was all about. By the time this gets to you I hope you're a million-billion times better, and Dr. Ruge[1] is going to keep Ed informed by wire all the time. I didn't want to scare your family until I knew what was going on, but have now sent Fred a night letter but explained that the crisis is past for fear he might get panic-stricken and scare your mother etc. Am also writing him airmail all the details, with the idea that that'll keep him from rushing right out there or anything of the sort.

I guess if you do want him or somebody to come out and see you safely back home when the time comes, he'd do it like a shot. But I know you've got to lie around and take it easy to get your strength back even when your fever has gone. Anyway, we really will do anything you want us to, and I'm writing Ruge to that effect right now. Ed is writing you and Ruge too, has wired Henry Hart (his

Henry Hart)[2] in Spokane to look out for you in the meanwhile, and really was so swell and upset all today that I'm very very fond of him. Everything on this end I'll take care of, including a letter about your storage warehouse bill I sent you Monday. So just try to sleep all the time and get well as fast and completely as you can. Maybe hospitals are the only place in the world where you can get that "peace" we've been trying to find you for so long. But I shouldn't kid about it because I'm honestly so damn sorry about it all that I don't know what to say.

Love, Nowell

1. Wolfe had fallen ill of pneumonia and was now under the care of Dr. E. C. Ruge, who had hospitalized him in his private sanitarium, Firlawns, twelve miles north of Seattle.

2. A Harvard professor of law who was a friend of Edward Aswell. His name was the same as that of a friend of Aline Bernstein.

114 East 56th Street
New York
July 15, 1938.

Listen, kid, take a tip from an old hand at hospitals and don't let the whole state of Washington come in to visit you. Because even though you're the kindest-hearted person in the whole wide world and can gather more friends per square inch per second than anybody I've ever seen, hospitals are to *rest* in, and the more you rest the quicker you'll be OK. I myself always hang a sign on my hospital door saying "Danger, beware of dog" or some such even when I have an ingrowing toenail removed. So you do it too!

Well, otherwise everything is calm here and I hope there likewise. I got a very nice letter from Mrs. Stevens[1] which I've sent down to Fred, although I guess somebody has written him or your mother direct from Seattle. The paper had a brief note in it saying you "had been sick," but I will hold back the crowd on this end if you'll get Dr. Ruge to do likewise on yours. (Am writing him my sentiments on the subject, so you needn't bother.)

I hope the hell it's cool out there as I think it is, instead of so muggy-hot as here. So you just stay there and take it easy, and tell Dr. Ruge or Mrs. S. or somebody to write me if you want anything— books, for instance, when you're strong enough to read. But don't you try to write any more until you're really 100% well. It wouldn't come out as good anyway and would only slow you down towards the time when you can go full-steam ahead. Gosh, I hope this doesn't sound as if I was bawling you out, but ever since I first heard about you I've been fighting back a temptation to come out there and sit at the foot of your bed with a double-barrelled shotgun for the benefit of all and sundry who try to come barging in unwanted. "Relax Is All" as Tess Slessinger called that story of hers, and so *I'd* better not write any more now for fear I myself will tire you. I can't help feeling so damn helpless to help you with all the U.S. between us, but you have somebody write me whatever you want, for my peace of mind if only that.

Lots of love
Nowell

PS Nice item for publishers anatomy. Reading Thoreau edited by HS Canby,[2] I find that HM made him pay for his first edition of Week on the Concord, and he had to peddle pencils from door to door for months and months, maybe even years, to pay for it! EN

1. In Seattle, Wolfe had been the guest of James Stevens, the novelist and compiler of Paul Bunyan stories. When Wolfe fell ill, he turned to Stevens and his wife for help, and Theresa Stevens recommended Dr. Ruge to him.

2. *The Works of Thoreau*, selected and edited by Henry Seidel Canby (Boston: Houghton Mifflin, 1937). Nowell's comment is inaccurate: Thoreau had to borrow money to pay to have *A Week on the Concord and Merrimac Rivers* published by James Munroe & Company. When the sale of the book did not meet the expense of publication, Thoreau took up surveying to discharge the debt.

[95 Madison St.
New Bedford, Mass.]
July 18, 1938

Dear Wolfe:

Bless you! I mean both in general and also for your "Out of the woods" telegram. I didn't know if you knew how seriously sick you were, and I didn't want to scare you while you were still "in the woods." So I tried to write fairly vague letters and sent them to Dr. Ruge in case you weren't well enough to read them.

Well anyway, there was a collective sigh of relief wafted over the whole New York area Friday night when Ed and I got your wires and began telephoning each other simultaneously long distance, each to be sure that the other had heard. I guess you're going to be as weak as a kitten, which will be pretty tough on anyone like you who always has gone fullsteam ahead, one hundred miles an hour. But anyway just take it easy and everything will be okay. As a matter of fact, I suddenly remembered that all those sense impressions, even the early ones under layers and layers of memory, come through more clearly, almost luminously when you are weak after being sick, at least I think so. So I hope that you can just lie still and sort of dream them without being impelled to write them down. They will stick with you even when you are better.

Well, in the meanwhile I have been having more or less correspondence with Fred and I am fonder of him than ever, because he has been so very swell about all this business. He wrote me a special delivery airmail asking my advice, saying that he could raise three or four hundred dollars and go right out there, or could send it to you in cash instead if I thought you needed it. I didn't like to tell him how much money I thought you had because I figured that might mean that some of the other members of the family would be touching you, and you ought to keep your own money more than ever now because of having been sick. So, anyway, I wrote Fred back and said that I didn't know the exact amount of money you had, but that I thought you had enough to cover the best medical care now and for him to just sit tight until you were well enough to tell him yourself whether you wanted him to come out or anything of the sort. By this time you will probably have wired him, and I guess you would probably convalesce more thoroughly and more in leisure if Fred doesn't go out there. But you just take your time and don't plan to come back until later on when you are really strong enough and also when New York is cooler. So, anyway, I will leave it up to whatever you think best, but I wanted to reassure you that I hadn't spilled the beans to the family about money either one way or another. Guess this is all for now except to explain that I am in New Bedford for the rest of this week, but Ed is going to phone me long distance, and Miss Krainin is to do likewise if any letters come from either Carolina or Seattle.

So just take it easy and let me know whatever you want, and lots of love in the meanwhile.

Sincerely,
Nowell

P.S. Sounds formal because a little New Bedburg stenog wrote it but anyway I'm so relieved and happy I hardly know what to say.

❧ ❧ ❧

114 East 56th Street
New York
July 26, 1938.

Dear Vulfe: (as Mrs. Mitchell[1] would say)

I haven't written you lately because I had an idea you shouldn't be bothered with too much mail, especially when it's a lot of petty detail of the kind I am so apt to write. Today, however, I got a note from nice Mrs. Stevens, telling me you were worried about Mr. Hannewald at the bank and Norman Kleinberg.[2] I called Hannewald and

he was very sorry to hear you were sick; said of course he would
leave matters exactly as they were and said he thought he might write
you—though nothing about business, because that was OK, but just
to tell you how sorry he was.

Norman already knew about you and was in a terrible dither last
week when that little note came out in the newspapers saying you
were sick. I swore Miss Jassinoff to secrecy because at that point you
were so sick that I didn't want you swamped with a lot of mail.
However, I talked to Norman myself on the phone and he too may
be going to write you. In the meanwhile, he says to tell you how
terribly sorry he is and that everything is all right. Miss Jassinoff
went and dug through your file to check up on the storage warehouse
business and was here today and says everything is in good order.
Norman would keep that stuff for the rest of his life. She says he is
terribly devoted to you and talked about nothing but what a swell
guy you were all the time she was with him, so everything is perfectly
under control. But if things start to worry you, just tell Mrs. Stevens
to write me so that I can get them off your chest. Please, kid, do be a
good boy and don't try to read, as Mrs. Stevens says you are dying
to. It's a good sign and I'm glad, but what the hell are you paying
nurses for, if they can't read aloud to you and give you your money's
worth? Books don't taste right when you read when you are sick
anyway, as you may have discovered by now if you do insist on
trying. I myself ("have you heard about my operation?") always
make Mother read to me. Maybe I'd better send her right out there
because that sing-song whoopsie-daisy voice of hers was guaranteed
to put me to sleep after at least one page or one sentence if it's Henry
Thoreau. In fact, she herself fell asleep a couple of times over Walden
right in the middle of a sentence. Maybe you ought to try it. It's
better than any kind of dope.

Guess this is all for now. Hope you and Fred are having a nice
quiet (!) time together.

Lots of Love,
Nowell

1. The cleaning woman for Wolfe's apartment at 865 First Avenue.
2. The bartender at the Chelsea Hotel, with whom Wolfe had left some of his
personal effects.

❦ ❦ ❦

114 East 56th Street
New York
August 4, 1938.

Dear Wolfe:

Well, Kid, I guess I've been neglecting you personally as far as correspondence goes, because I wasn't sure if you were well enough to have letters, so spent most of my time writing back and forth to Fred and Mrs. Stevens, etc. Ed and I have now got the news that you are really and truly convalescing and boy, I certainly feel like a million dollars now that it's all over, except the getting back your strength. Maybe I ought to get tough here and try to put the fear of God into you by saying *don't* you go kiting off to anywhere until Ruge tells you that it really is absolutely OK for you to exert yourself that much. It's only natural for you to be pretty damn weak and easily exhausted for a good while after you really are considered cured, and the less you use up that fund of strength, the quicker said fund will pile itself up to the almost super-human endurance that you used to have and that you will be trying on again when you get back to working on the book. In other words, easy does it; so be a good boy and keep on relaxing.

Well, kid, here is a bunch of mail which just came for you. I have made notes on the envelope of each, telling you whether I answered them, etc., although I got a nice letter from Mrs. Armstrong[1] saying she hopes you would be OK, so am writing back to reassure her now. Also, the usual from Cane, but I am writing to explain about your sickness which ought to hold the s.o.b., if he has one drop of human kindness in him. In other words, everything is completely under control, so take it easy in every way.

I guess maybe Fred will have left by the time this reaches you, but if not, give him my love and explain that I didn't answer his last because I thought he might be gone by the time it reached there.

Well, kid, you now have gone through another kind of human experience anyway, so what the hell—maybe it will do no harm in the long run as long as you are coming out of it with such flying colors, but take it easy, don't forget.

Love,
Nowell

[P.S.] My! I see that every paragraph, practically, begins with "Well, kid" but the phone kept ringing. Anyway—"kid"—I'm so damn glad it IS well!

1. Anne Armstrong had met Wolfe in Bristol, Tennessee, in the spring of 1937. She later offered to rent him a mountain cabin near Bristol. Her memoir, "As I Saw Thomas Wolfe," was published in the *Arizona Quarterly*, Spring 1946.

❦ ❦ ❦   August 9, 1938

THOMAS WOLFE CARE DR. E C RUGE
1424 FOURTH AVE SEATTLE WASH
TAKE IT EASY KID I KNOW ITS TERRIBLY TOUGH FOR YOU
NOW BECAUSE SO SUDDEN AND UNACCUSTOMED BUT IF
YOULL ONLY PROMISE ME TO REST I WILL PROMISE YOU
THAT THE BOOK WILL COME OUT BETTER AND RIPER AND
EASIER IN THE END ED AGREES BOTH WRITING LOTS OF
LOVE

                    NOWELL

❦ ❦ ❦   114 East 56th Street
                                         New York
                                         August 10, 1938.

Dear Wolfe:

I sat right down and sent you that telegram as soon as I got news from Mrs. Stevens about the spot on your lung.[1] I'm not sure exactly what I said now that it's morning, because I just wanted first of all to say how damned sorry I was, and to try to reassure you that things would still be OK in spite of it. It occurred to me to-day that I may have sounded too damn Pollyanna-ish about it—that you may have thought when you read it "Sure, that's OK for Nowell to promise me the book will be better and riper and easier. Sure but she takes the whole thing pretty lightly." Well, I wouldn't blame you, but I honestly and truly *do* think what I wired about the book.

I guess what made it pop into my mind chiefly was remembering how easily "Child By Tiger," for instance, came out. And my exclaiming about it and your saying "I've had that in my mind for a long time." But "Child By Tiger" or no "Child By Tiger" it's always lurked in the back of my mind that you caused yourself a lot [of] grief and physical exhaustion in writing by sort of thinking on paper —you know, starting a thing and then thinking of something else that maybe went with it, then weaving that in etc. Sure, I guess it's the old web, and I admit it gives a book the richness and all the things that you're known for. But MAYbe—well, here goes Pollyanna again—this sickness business will sort of force you through physical circumstances to learn an easier, more premeditated way to work. But think it over and give it a try. You'll have to now anyway unless you want to be a plain damn fool and make getting well a long long, even maybe doubtful process, by forcing yourself when you're not well enough. But try thinking things out, over and over, lying around and who can tell—it may work out swell and save you all that torture of work in the end?????

Well, I'm damned if I know how this will strike you. Because God knows, you know the workings of your own creative processes better than I could ever hope to. But you never can tell till you try, so try anyway both because of necessity and because it may work out swell.

But DO, please, realize the necessity of behaving yourself. Because I've had that on my mind ever since I saw the photo Fred sent me with you in the background. You looked so sort of—well, disgruntled is the best word I can think of, that I didn't know whether to laugh or to cry. I know almost all men, especially healthy men, are like that about getting sick, whereas women are used to it and instinctively just give in to it and sort of sleep it off. But even at the risk of insulting your manhood or some such, I can't help playing the same old tune over and over in every letter: "Relax is all: don't fight it, just give in to it and it'll get over with all the sooner. Rest and rest until you feel the old fight welling up inside you—and even though it sometimes seems it never will, it suddenly starts fizzing around and everything is swell." Naturally I can't start comparing my minor illnesses with this whole business of yours. But honest, kid, rest is the cure-all for EVERYTHING, take Gorki, for instance. He had TB for thirty-to-fifty years and never got cured of it the way you can from this one spot if you just behave. But because he had horse sense enough to take care of himself he was able to write for a whole long rich life, and I guess he'd still be alive now if they hadn't poisoned him as the only way to bump him off. But he went to Capri or wherever it was and did absolutely nothing for a while. So do please be a good boy and go thou to Palo Alto[2] and do likewise.

Well, kid, come to think of it, I suspect that almost all the great Russian writers had a spot of it at some time or another didn't they? So maybe it's a good, typical literary disease. But from what I can gather, you really won't have it unless you try to drag yourself around and do too much, and sleep and eat wrong and do everything wrong, the way you're apt to. When I think of it, I just plain want to tie you to my apronstrings and see that you go to bed, and eat three square meals a day, and live like other people, instead of driving yourself and driving yourself and wasting an equivalent of time wandering round on trains looking for "peace" and rest and never getting it. God knows, you've got a basically superhuman-strong physique or you never could have got away with it all these years. So just try to think of this as if you were an engine and just needed to have your valves ground and carbon removed?????

Gosh, I certainly am rambling on and on, but I sort of can't help it. Because I can imagine you kicking and kicking against the pricks, as stubborn as a mule, and it makes me sad and sore and everything all at once. I honestly think that being sick gracefully and with a strong kind of fatalistic acceptance is an accomplishment that people learn. So try to learn it anyway, just on my say-so. And maybe you'll even turn into a hospital-dipsomaniac like me—though it's kind of hard to imagine from the bellicose look on your face in that photo. But if you can only learn it you'll be 50% cured. Honest. I believe it practically fanatically. And considering I was sposed to die almost any minute from the age of 1 hour to 10 years, I think I really am a pretty swell example of how tough a person can get to be with patience???? Or am I blowing my own horn here too damn much?

Well, kid, just one more thing, and then Pollyanna-Florence-Night-ingale-Mary-Baker-Eddy will sign off. That is, an idea that struck me against the time when you do feel the old fight beginning to bubble around inside of you. I'm talking out of turn, but I THINK the chances are very very swell that Harper's would be only too delighted if you decided later to finish up the Western Journal and let them publish that ahead of the big novel. From idle conversations with Ed I gathered that he thought that sounded swell, and I do think you could work on that much sooner than pouring your whole soul and energy and "life's-blood" as you used to say into The Web and The Rock. So I've written Ruge and asked him if he and the Palo Alto doctor don't think maybe later, when you really begin to get raring to go, you could dictate a *little* (really little—say an hour or so a day, but with time out for meals and sleep and rest like a human being).

I guess it's too early in the game for them to promise anything definite, what with the pneumonia still hovering around, or leaving it's shadow behind it, or however it is. But sort of turn it over in your mind and see if you think it wouldn't be a good idea. Or, hell, we've got enough stories for a book of those right this minute, without your doing a damn thing except telling me to start collecting 'em and send you a list for approval. So don't, honestly, worry. You've got one book ready to come out at any time. You've got the western journal to work on leisurely and without exhaustion when the time is ripe as it's bound to be soon *if you behave*. And by that time, you'll probably be tougher than ever and raising more hell. Look at our mutual friend Mr. K. S. Crichton, for instance, even though he had it very very seriously and really has only one lung worth writing home about.

So, whoa! I'm trying to catch myself before I get Pollyannaing again. God knows whether this will only make you sore, thinking I don't realize how miserable you feel. Or maybe you really will see some horse sense in it, at least in parts of it???? So do please try to take it all as easy as you can. Don't stew, don't worry, don't drive yourself. Just lie around, and if and whenever you want me to pop the idea of stories or the western journal to Ed, just tell me to or let me do it just as a friend or something like that.

Lots of love, and sympathy, Pollyannaing or no,

Nowell

P.S. Am sending this care of Ruge, because I'm not sure whether you're back at Firlawns, still in x-ray hospital, starting to Palo Alto, or what—

1. Because Wolfe's convalescence from the pneumonia was attended by recurrent fever and headache, he underwent further medical and X-ray examination at the Providence Hospital in Seattle and a spot on his lung was discovered. It was later identified as a tubercular lesion that had healed sometime early in his life but had now been activated by the pneumonia.

2. Wolfe had planned to visit his friend Dr. Russel Lee in Palo Alto, California, and continue his recovery there.

114 East 56th Street
New York
August 12, 1938.

Dear Wolfe:

I think maybe I wrote that Tuesday letter a little bit half-cocked. I mean I didn't understand from Mrs. Stevens' letter and thought that they were afraid you really did have a T.B. infection of some kind, even though not the whole hog of tuberculosis. Since then, I've got a very nice letter from Ruge giving me all the dirt on the situation, and boy, I certainly do feel a million times relieved to hear that the lung specialist thinks maybe you haven't got it, although you evidently must have had it sometime or other and cured yourself by some miraculous process. I remember now reading somewhere that almost everybody had a little T.B. at some time or other and threw it off; and I hope that that was what it was with you and that it's only the pneumonia business which stirred things up a speck. Well, I guess time will prove pretty definitely that you are OK, but I still do wish the hell that you would promise to take no chances and take things very very easy so we can be sure.

Ruge says it will only take six weeks to two months and that honestly is practically no time at all—certainly as far as the book goes. For instance, you've laid off writing for much much longer periods than that when you were in Germany, or even in Asheville, or even on this trip to the Pacific, before you got sick. I guess you don't realize how fast time goes when you do get travelling; so the two months don't seem like time wasted to you because you don't realize they are going by. But honest, try to remember that two months, even when they are forced upon you, are after all only two months—so what the hell. Besides, I don't want to put any ideas in your head, but as you yourself have said so many times: "It's all grist in the mill, so what the hell." Well, guess this is all for now and hope this isn't too Pollyanna. I realize it's sort of hard for you to see it in the rosy light I do because you are sick and sad and damn impatient, but it really won't be long, I promise you, so cheer up all you can.

Enclosed, a note from a gentleman named Mr. Muller,[1] announcing that you can get high balls for 6¢ a piece in Mexico, and other interesting items. I opened it in case it was anything I' ought to answer, but after reading it, decided I better not write the guy for fear he might feel funny about having had some strange skirt read all this personal stuff—the anecdote—burros and burras, etc. Also Arthur Mann[2] called up to ask how you were getting on and to find out if you were well enough to be getting letters. I told him to write care of Dr. Ruge, because I wasn't sure which hospital you were at. And so I guess this is all for now, except lots of love.

                                                      Nowell

1. Professor Herbert Muller, one of Wolfe's hosts during the Purdue visit, later wrote the first book-length critical study of Wolfe's work, *Thomas Wolfe* (New York: New Directions, 1947).

2. A sports writer and radio broadcaster whom Wolfe had come to know through his interest in baseball.

❦   ❦   ❦

                                          114 East 56th Street
                                          New York
                                          August 30, 1938.
Dear Wolfe:

I guess you'll think I've been deserting you. I wrote you care of Dr. Lee, thinking you'd be showing up there, but then I heard the latest about you're having got some more fever, and have been trying to get a chance ever since to write you and say how sorry I was. I gather now that you're over it and I HONestly think the worst is over now. So anyway, my letter in care of Lee wasn't anything important—mostly quotes from Thoreau as I remember it now, plus the usual admonitions to be a good boy, to take it easy etc. He wrote back a nice note explaining that you'd been delayed but seemed quite cheerful at the prospect of your really getting completely strong and well and not having to stay with him and forego writing as long as

I'd thought when that silly TB scare was in the air. So cheer up, kid, it won't be long now.

Well, it certainly looks as if you'd been having a good deal of excitement of the changing of doctors and all.[1] But I think Fred was dead right, and I'm only sorry you had to be made miserable about it all. Got a very noble letter from Ruge saying that he'd stepped out of the case because he thought it was best to avoid confusion etc. He didn't say that he'd been asked to step out, and I didn't let on that I knew. I wrote him a letter saying I agreed with him that it was best and I wanted to thank him for his magnanimity in doing so. But I was very careful not to say anything that he could construe as meaning I wished he was still on the case. Have sent a copy of my letter to Mabel[2] just to be sure Ruge doesn't misrepresent it to you or her. I *was* very polite because I figured best to smoothe his ruffled pride, if any, and have it all end with good feeling and "peace." He kept saying how devoted he was to you, and I guess the guy was as far as his limitations would let him be. But somehow psychologists always seem to be or to get to be queer birds, and you've got enough trouble of your own without having to cope with anybody's temperament while you're trying to get strong.

So anyway, it's all over now, and I hope and pray that you really WILL be enjoying the long-longed-for peace by the time this gets out there to you. Everything here is quiet as a mill pond, no gossip or anything to report. Miss Jassinoff got a job with Dell Publications on one of their movie magazines. But she is properly and typically snooty and funny about it. So the chances are that you could wean her away from it with a crook of your little finger if you want her back later. Though in the meanwhile she'll have plenty of dough to get along on, and is planning to go to night school to learn shorthand which she should have learned way back. She's a swell girl and terribly funny when she's not trying to be "efficient" as she puts it. Her saga of interviews for possible jobs this summer is enough to make a horse laugh, especially when told with her kind of bitter mimicry. But I won't spoil it by trying to tell it, but will let her tell you sometime when you're back here.

As for me, I'm just pushing along as usual. With more damn work and I don't know what for exactly. I got pretty pooped with the hot weather and went home for 10 days, so now feel pretty swell, though am going home again for Labor Day weekend and my old Nana's 35th anniversary since she came to work for the crazy Nowells the year before I was born. But I'll be back here Tuesday the 6th anyway, so any letters from Mabel or anyone will reach me OK.

Well, kid, this isn't very exciting or interesting to you, so I guess I may as well sign off for now. But anyway the main point was just to say that I'm rooting for you and hoping you're really raring to go, rid of the fever and everything by now. You won't be literally "rarin'" for a while yet because it takes a hell of a long while for anybody whose been sick like that to get all their strength back. But try to be as patient as you can, the worst is over, honest, and so just wait patiently a little longer and you'll feel all the old pep boiling up inside of you again.

Love,
Nowell

1. Dr. Ruge and the two physicians he had called in for consultation were in disagreement about Dr. Ruge's diagnosis that the spot on the lung was a tubercular lesion. As a result, Wolfe and his brother Fred discharged Dr. Ruge and retained his colleague, Dr. Charles Watts.

2. Mabel Wheaton, Wolfe's sister, who had by now traveled to Seattle to take care of her brother.

When Wolfe's fever and headaches continued and he began to have episodes of slight irrationality, Dr. Watts and later Dr. George Swift, a brain specialist who had been invited into the case by Harper's, suspected a brain abscess and recommended that Wolfe be sent to Johns Hopkins Hospital in Baltimore. After exploratory brain surgery at the Johns Hopkins Hospital, Dr. Walter Dandy discovered that a long dormant tubercular lesion in Wolfe's lung had reopened as a result of the pneumonia and the tubercular bacilli had been carried by the bloodstream to his brain. His case was hopeless. He died in Baltimore on September 15, 1938. Elizabeth Nowell was at the hospital in Baltimore and helped to comfort the members of the family during Wolfe's last hours.

"No More Rivers"

As the letters have indicated, Wolfe and Nowell had two kinds of difficulty with "No More Rivers." The major difficulty was with Maxwell Perkins, who objected, first, to having a Scribner editor, Wallace Meyer, be an easily recognized figure in the story and, second, to Wolfe's including satirical vignettes that reflected upon Charles Scribner, upon Whitney Darrow, the business manager, upon Robert Bridges, the retired editor of Scribner's Magazine, *and upon other members of the firm.*

Miss Nowell describes in some detail the negotiations she carried out at the Scribner office:

> I discussed the Scribner material at length with Perkins: Tom sent me in to CSS with No More Rivers and told me to find out how Perkins and Meyer reacted to it. Perkins sat stubbornly in his office and refused to give it to Meyer—said I would have to do it, he didn't want anything to do with it. So I did, and went back a few days later to get the reaction. Meyer laughed it off and was very nice about it. Said it was all right with him but he wished he knew who all those beautiful women with husky voices were who supposedly called him up. But I think he was really upset. The truth was, as somebody, I guess Perkins, told me afterwards, that Meyer's girl had not given him the air but had very suddenly and tragically died, and that that was why he'd gone into his shell. Charlie Scribner didn't enter into the discussion of the Scribner material at all with me, and if he had been terribly upset, I should think he would have.
>
> Anyway, the only person who was upset, to my knowledge, was Perkins himself, and his whole complaint was personal . . . that he had told Tom most of the facts about Scribner's and Scribner people, in confidence, and that if Tom exaggerated and satirized them and wrote them up, he would feel it was his duty to resign.[1]

Under these circumstances, Wolfe was persuaded to revise the story. He dropped the satirical vignettes about the Scribner people and he made the main character, George Hauser, a piano teacher instead of a publisher's reader.[2] With Miss Nowell's help, he also reduced the story from sixty-three to thirty-four pages.

*But the characterization of George Hauser posed a second diffi-
culty. Wolfe was attempting to present him as a very repressed
personality yet at the same time to give him feelings of rich response
to the life of the city and to the scenes of his boyhood in Minnesota.
He was not successful in blending these two contradictory elements
in the characterization. In fact, one might say that he gave his
character the soul of a Eugene Gant and the habit patterns of an
orderly, fussy person who feared life. This situation no doubt
contributed to the problems Miss Nowell had in getting the story
published.*

*When Wolfe revised his story, he had satisfied, it seemed, Perkins's
objections, for Perkins read the new version and pronounced that it
could not harm anyone now except Wolfe himself. Magazine editors,
on the other hand, deemed it would not appeal to the general reader,
and Miss Nowell peddled it around for a year and a half without
success. Finally, just before Wolfe's death Helen McAfee of the* Yale
Review *accepted the story. But she wanted some words or phrases
altered and some long passages about the river and American life
cut out.*

*These requests for changes after Wolfe's death led ultimately to
Perkins's having his way in blocking publication. Miss Nowell
explains what happened:*

> Miss McAfee was a fussy old maid and some of the changes
> she wanted to make ruined the rhythm of the story. Also some
> of her requested changes called for some actual new writing. I
> sent her list of requested changes and the manuscript to Perkins,
> who was then Tom's executor, and wrote him saying that I had
> no right to write in any actual passages under Tom's name, and
> what would we do? I thought that he might write the passages
> in himself. But he answered that "under the circumstances" he
> thought we would have to call the whole thing off. I think he
> had a right to do this but I think he did it with too great alacrity
> and relief and that it was really wrong.[3]

*Since "No More Rivers" is the earliest example of a new develop-
ment in Wolfe's writing, it has considerable interest for any reader of
Wolfe's work. Besides the evocative passages about the morning
traffic on the East River, about the freight cars of the American railroads, and about the landscape of the upper reaches of the Mississippi, it shows us Wolfe's experimenting with the consciousness of a
man who was totally different from himself and doing so sympatheti-
cally. It represents a transition in 1936 toward the creation of*

George Webber as the mature, more restrained man of feeling in You
Can't Go Home Again. *It is good to have it in print at last.*

1. Letter to Edward Aswell, November 20, 1953, Elizabeth Nowell Papers, Houghton Library.

2. Edward Aswell eventually used some of this material when he was constructing
You Can't Go Home Again, in Chapter 2, pp. 21–27.

3. Letter to Edward Aswell, November 20, 1953, Elizabeth Nowell Papers, Houghton Library.

No More Rivers
by Thomas Wolfe

George awoke at seven-thirty, and for a moment lay flat on his back, and listened to the beating of his heart. With the fingers of one hand, he felt his pulse, and counted: "one-two-three-four"—the great pump beat regularly enough, until "five-six-seven"—blank terror filled him—it had jumped a beat! Great God, it had fluttered for a moment like a wing—now it missed again!—fluttered—beat again —George pressed hot fingers on his wrist and listened. He was sick with fear! His pulse now beat like a sledgehammer in his throat, it pounded thickly, like the muffled beating of a bell in his eardrums. Gradually, it subsided: his pulse beat regularly again, until the convulsion of his fear had passed. His pleasant face resumed its normal quietness.

I have heard, thought George, that it may miss *two* strokes, and yet the man will live. I have even heard it said that it can miss *three* strokes, and *still* the man can live. But I have heard it said that if it misses *four*—the man is dead, the heart will never beat again.

Oh God, he thought, as the agony of horror filled his soul again— to be composed of so much bitter agony, such lust of living and such fear of dying, that all the oceans of the world could never hold the huge unfathomed sum of it, and all of it dependent for its life upon the beating of a tired pump!

One-two-three-four! It's just a little pump, yet it can never stop— if it should stop for half a minute, we are gone. Great God, do people *know*? Do they never stop to think about the terror of the heart?— that small, frail pulse of pumping blood that is the only thing that stands between them—all they have and strive for and accomplish— and blank nothingness?

Do they never lie alone in this great city as I have lain alone here many thousand times—and listen to the beating of their hearts?

Do they not know that really there is nothing in the world but— *heart*? That this whole enormous city is nothing but heart?—that the lives of all men living are nothing more than just the beating of a heart?

Have they never lain here in darkness thinking of these things? Have they never lain here at night in all their little rooms—their wretched rabbit-warrens of brick, their dizzy battlements of stone, tier above tier and floor upon floor? In seven million little cells of men, and in these seven million little cells of men, are seven million little pumps, all beating in the seven million cells of night, all joining seven million heartbeats to the heart of sleep, all uniting to the single beating of the city's heart?

Have they never *counted*? Have they never *listened*? Have they never heard them in the night, as I have heard them all so many times, giving their pulse to sleep and silence and the flowing of the river, ticking like tiny clocks the promise of their pulse to—death?

He lay still on his couch and listened to the steady rumble of the traffic on First Avenue, just half a block away—the heavy rattling of the huge trucks rumbling down to get their morning load; and the smooth, thrumming, projectile-like precision of the motor cars. He had seen it all a thousand times—huge rusty trucks, the gaudy taxis flashing past; huge limousines, or motors of a common make, or speedy roadsters driven by assured young men, driving to their offices from their country homes.

And oh, the certitude, the alert and daring *will* of all these people: —all flashing past with this same overwhelming confidence that faced the swarming complex of the city's life—but did *they* know? Did *they* know that this invincible will of purpose—that the whole of this gigantic energy—was dependent on the frail, uncertain beating of a heart?

And all these other ones—those unnumbered motes of life who now were being hurled into this tortured rock through tunnels roaring with the blind velocity of the subway trains, who were roaring in across the bridges, rushing in by train, sliding in packed in a dense wall across the blunted snouts of ferries—who were pouring out of seven million sleeping cells in all the dense compacted warrens of the city life, to be rushed to seven million other *waking* cells of work— did *they* know? They were being hurtled in from every spot upon the compass—the crack trains of the nation were crashing up from Georgia, flashing down out of New England, the crack trains thirty coaches long that had smashed their way all night across the continent—from Chicago, from St. Louis, from Montreal, Atlanta, New Orleans, and Texas. These great projectiles of velocity that had bridged America with the pistoned stroke, the hot and furious breath of their terrific drive, were now pounding at the river's edge upon the very lintels of the city. They were filled with people getting up—at sixty miles an hour—filled with people getting dressed—at sixty miles an hour—filled with people getting shaved—at sixty miles an hour—walking down carpeted narrow aisles between the green baize curtains of the Pullman berths—at sixty miles an hour—and sitting down to eat substantial breakfasts in splendid windowed dining cars, while the great train smashes at the edges of that noble wink, the enchanted serpent of the Hudson River. The hot breath of the tremendous locomotive fairly pants against the lintels of the terrific city —all at sixty miles an hour—and all for *what?* for *what?*—Great God, that all these people, dressed and shaved and breakfasted, and hurled halfway across the continent by night—might add, each in his own way, their little sum to the gigantic total of that universal agony! Didn't they ever ask themselves *why* they should get up in the morning at all, *why* they should dress, and gulp down coffee, and then rush out into the streets with a look of grim determination in their eye, to push and be pushed, dodge and scuttle across, be hurled through tunnels and come swarming, clawing their way out of them —for what? for *what?*—So that they could get from one ridiculous little cell where they slept, to another ridiculous cell where they worked, and go about doing ridiculous things all day long— writing ridiculous letters, making or receiving ridiculous telephone calls, "getting in touch" (which was itself ridiculous, how? why? should you try to "get in touch" with anyone)—with other ridiculous people, looking up ridiculous things in a filing cabinet, or filing them away. Good Lord, couldn't they see that all of it was a spectacle to make the men on Mars—if men on Mars existed—split their sides with laughter? Couldn't they see that everything began with and returned to the only thing for which they should care at all—the frail uncertain beating of a—*heart!*

For him, at any rate, that had become the only thing for which he cared—to keep his own heart beating, to avoid in every way he could the brutal shocks of life and business, of speed, confusion, noise, and violence, of love, of grief, of happiness and heartbreak! Great God! Would people never *learn?* Would they never understand that the frail and naked heart could not be used as a football, kicked about by all the brutal and indifferent feet of life? Oh, if he could only tell them how slight a thing it took to plunge the anguish of a cureless hurt into the heart's deep core—how slight a thing—a tread upon the stairs, the intonation of a voice, the opening of a door—could fill the heart with joy and anguish—if he could only tell them how slight a thing it took to make hearts break!

Therefore, no more, no more! For him, at any rate, his care henceforth would be to keep his heart in one small cell, and so to spare his heart and hearts of other people. No more to dare adventure, or to risk defeat with this frail heart! No more to endure the agony of grief, the cureless pain of loss, the insane devotion, and the wound remediless of love! No more friendship; no more love and no more hatred, no more conflict, no more desire, no more happiness, no more men and no more women.

No more streets! He heard again the heavy thunder of the traffic on First Avenue; again he saw that violence of speed and hot machinery—but no more streets!

George turned his head, and for a moment looked about the room with tired eyes. In the cool sweet light of early morning his beautiful little apartment was spotless as a pin. He did not have much furniture: a table or two, a few good chairs, designed in the clean planes and angles of the modern fashion. There was a fireplace with a small clock upon the mantel and over it a long panoramic photograph of a noble river, with grand spacial vistas of high buttes and grandly wooded shores.

The piece that dominated the room was George's grand piano, a shining shape of grace and power; his face softened and he smiled a little as he looked at it. Then he reached out of bed and got his glasses, adjusted them, and began to read the memorandum that lay beside him on the table.

The schedule of the day's activity lay neatly mapped out before him in the pages of the little leather book. Mr. Robert Carpenter was due at ten o'clock; Mr. Milton Weisenborn at eleven; Mr. John Michael Leahy at noon. He began again at two o'clock when he received Mr. Tony Bertillotti; Mr. Peter Jorgensen at three; and Mr. Joseph Silverstein, perhaps the most talented of all his students, at four.

This was his program for the day. He was a teacher to young pianists who had shown distinguished promise and who were studying with a view to appearances on the concert stage. That had also been his own life formerly—before he had found out about his heart.

It was funny that no one had ever told him about the heart. He had known some of the most eminent people, he had studied under some of the ablest teachers—they had warned him about all sorts of things, but none of them had ever spoken of the heart.

If someone, in all those years of study and of preparation, had only told him a few very simple, fundamental things. If someone had only told him that before playing he would always feel not ready. If they'd only told him that he'd always feel—no matter how many times he practised—that if he only had one more day he'd be sure that he'd be ready to play the piece. If someone, out of all his teachers, in all the weary years of grinding and incessant practice, had only told him of some way in which he could feel *sure* of what he knew, of some way in which he could control his nerves—so that his subconscious mind would take him through!

But no one had ever told him—George glanced swiftly, briefly, at his wrist watch and then again at the little leather notebook of his day's schedule, before he closed it—and he had come to this!

If only someone had told him what to do when he got out there upon the stage to play, when he saw out in the huge dark pool of the great house that disembodied host of faces blooming there in the darkness, white, innumerable, like petals on a bough, when space, time, everything is gone. If someone had only told him what to do when he first sat down at the piano, how to conquer the nervousness that made him feel as if he'd lost control of the muscles of his hands. It's true he had talked about this to many other people, to concert pianists far better known than himself, and all of them were full of bland encouragements. They would all assure him that he would "find" himself when he struck the first chords. They would assure him that as time went on he would get calmer and surer, that after the first applause he would feel much better, that encores were always the *best* because a musician is surer of himself by then and not nervous and in "a more exalted frame of mind."

Yes, they had told him this, but it had not worked out according to their telling. His pulse had always beaten like a trip hammer, and his heart had kept time until it seemed the heart strings would be torn right out of him, until it seemed that nothing was worth this agony, no effort, no applause was worth the terror and the peril of this ordeal—until there was nothing left for him in all his consciousness, except that ghastly choking beating of the heart. And so—no more! —no more!—let others dare the ordeal if they liked, let others tempt the perilous, stricken beating of the frail small heart—but as for him—well, he had come to this. And this was better.

George looked at his wrist watch. It was eight-fifteen. He got up, put on his slippers and a dressing gown, took off his gold-rimmed spectacles, and polished them carefully, and put them on again. Without his glasses, his face had the slightly tired, patient look that is common among people with weak eyes. With his glasses on, the expression of his face was somewhat changed: it was a pleasant, most attractive face, well-modelled, firm, distinguished by a look of quiet strength and natural gentleness, all subdued somehow to the suggestive hue of a tranquil but deep-rooted melancholy. It would have been hard for a stranger to believe that this man could be the slave of an obsession, could hold in him such ocean depths of terror, such dread of everything that might disturb the frail small beating of the heart.

George walked over to the windows, pulled up the shutters of one Venetian blind, and for a moment stood looking quietly out upon the river. Everything was touched with morning, and the river was flashing with all the ecstasy and movement of its thousand currents.

A cool breath of morning, sea-fresh, and tide-laden, curiously half-rotten, flowed over his calm features: that living river and its smell, he understood, was like all life. The river was a flowing sewer surging back and forth to the recession of the tides, and bearing in its tainted flood the excremental dumpings of six million men. And yet the river was a tide of flashing life, marked delicately in a hundred places with the silvery veining of a hundred currents, and pungent with the vital, aqueous, full salt-laden freshness of the sea.

The tide was coming in upon the full; George stood there, watching quietly, and saw it come. It was a steady, flowing, crawling and impulsive surge—a welling flood that would come on forever and knew no limit to the invasion of its power. The river was not quiet; the tide was ruffled by the breath of morning into a million scallop-shells of winking light—rose, golden, silver, sapphire, pink—the whole polychrome of morning was reflected in the stream, and within the channel of the river's life, the tide came on.

Morning, shining morning, filled the river, and transformed the town. Across the river the tormented visage of Long Island City had also been transformed; that grim forest of smokestacks, chimneys, enormous stamped-out factory moulds, million-windowed warehouses, gas tanks and refineries, derricks, tugboats, cranes and docks, was magically translated by the wizardry of every hue that morning knows.

As he looked, a tug, set neatly in between two barges, each loaded with twin rows of box-cars, backed out into the stream and quartered slowly, steadily, with its enormous freight, then started head-on up the stream. Thick water foamed against the blunt snouts of the barges, as the little tug between them neatly forged ahead with its great cargo, with a sense of limitless power, and with astonishing speed. The young cool light of morning fell flat and cleanly on the rusty sides of the old freight cars on the barges: everything began to blaze with thrilling color. The excitement, the beauty, the feelings of wonder and recognition which all the associations of the scene evoked, were intoxicating. It was not just the composition of the scene itself; the thing that made the heart beat faster, and the throat get tight, and something stab as swift and instant as a knife—was not so much the beauty and the wonder of the thing as the beauty and wonder which the thing evoked. The little tug was not just a little tug that plied about the waters of Manhattan. No, the little tug was sliding lights at night—red, yellow, green, as hard and perfect as cut gems, as poignant, small, and lonely as the hearts of men. The little tug was like the lights of darkness in America, which stretch across the continent like strung beads, which are so brave, so small, so lonely in that huge vacancy of the attentive and eternal dark. The tug was like dark waters of the night, the poignant lights that slide there in the viewless dark, down past the huge cliff of the silent and terrific city, the eyes of the unnumbered windows, the huge heart of the city, and the small beating hearts of sleep.

The little tug was like the evocation of those things, it was like the great piers blazing in the night at twelve o'clock, the dense packed crowds, the rattling winches, and the lighted ship. It was like the huge turmoil of departure, the shattering blast of the great ship, the great hawsers straining, taut as thrumming wires, as twelve small bull-dog tugs heave back and get their teeth in, haul her out and straighten her into the stream, until the liner's terrific side turns flat and level to Manhattan. Her lights blaze up from her sheer side, nine rows of light across one thousand feet of length, the proud sweep of all her storied promenades, the great white curve of all her super-structure, breasted like a swan, the racing slant and spurt of the great funnels, the whole thing sliding past the city now. At twelve-fifteen, the funnels show along the piers at the end of Eleventh Street, the people in old red-brick houses down in Greenwich Village see the lights slide past. At twelve-fifteen the Berengaria moans, the tugs cut loose, the lighted cliff of the great liner slides past the lighted cliff of the great city, seeks the Narrows, finds the sea. And the tug was like the evocation of these things.

The enormous barges spoke, as did the tugs, of the huge traffic of the harbor, of docks and piers and loadings, of the raw use and labor of America. But more than anything else the barges belonged to sunset; they belonged to the vast hush of evening, the old-gold of the setting sun that burns the fiery furnace of its last radiance in one pane of glass high up in the great splinter of a sky-scraper, or in one pane of glass there in a warehouse of Long Island City. The barges, then, belonged to evening and to sunset, and America. They belonged to the sense of vast completion, the sense of mighty labor ended, the huge and quiet respiration of the tired earth. The barges belonged to all the men who lean upon the sills of evening in America, and regard with quiet eyes, and know that night is coming, labor done. The barges belong to all the quiet waters of the evening, to the vast and empty hush of piers, to quiet waters that come in with quiet glut, to slap against old crusted pilings of the wharves, to slap against the sides of rusty barges tethered there, to rock them gently, and to bump their rusty sides together, stiffly to rock the high poles of the derrick-booms. The old barges belonged to all these things, to sunset and the end of work, and to the long last fading slants of light here in America that will fall, like sorrow and an unknown joy, upon the old red brick of houses, so to lie there briefly like the ghost of light and so to wane, to die there, knowing night has come.

As for the freight cars, they were companion to these things, and they belonged to all the rest of it as well. Even their crude raw color —a color of dried ox-blood, grimed and darkened to the variation of their age—seemed to have been derived from some essential pigment of America, somehow to express the whole weather of her life. George looked at them and saw their faded lettering: he could not read it, but he knew that if he could, he would find the names of most of the great lines of the nation—the Pennsylvania, and the New York Central, The Erie, Lackawanna, and New Haven, the Baltimore and Ohio, the Southern, the North Western, and the Santa Fe.

He knew that those iron wheels had pounded back and forth along almost every mile of rail whose giant web covered the country. He knew that those harsh ox-blood frames of wood and steel had been exposed to every degree and every violence of weather the continent knows. He knew that they had broiled in train yards out in Kansas, all through the sweltering afternoons of mid-July, when the temperature stood at 107°. He knew that they had been beaten upon with torrential rain, frozen over in a six-inch sheath of ice and snow; he knew that in the night-time they had toiled their way, behind the thundering bellows of a "double header," up through the sinuous grades of the Appalachians, or pounded their way by day, straight as a string across the plains of western Kansas. They had crossed the Mississippi and the Rio Grande; they had known the lonely barren pine lands of the South, as well as the towering forests of the great Northwest; they had known the cornlands, crossed the plains, gone round or through the Rocky Mountains; they had crossed the blasted fiend-world of Nevada, and they had sought and found the great Pacific shore. He had thundered past unending strings of them, lined up across the midlands of the country, and he had seen them for a fleeting instant from the windows of a speeding train, curved back upon a spur of rusty track in lonely pine lands of the South, at red and waning sunset in the month of March, open and deserted, yet indefinably thrilling, filled somehow with all the wildness, loneliness, the message of enormous distance, that is America.

George turned away from the window with a faint sigh—not so much the sigh of a man who is physically tired, but of one whose weariness has sunk deep into all the secret places of his life. That flashing tide that never ceased was no more for him to be experienced or endured. The living energy of all its veined and weaving currents, the constant traffics of its multi-form and never-ending life—with all their evocations of the violence of living—was no more to be endured. Hereafter, one small cell surrounded by his careful walls was all that he desired. There would be no more rivers in the life of George.

As he turned away from the window, the look of melancholy in his quiet face was more marked than it had ever been, but in a moment he stirred himself and set about his preparations for the day.

He went about each task with a sense of order that never varied in its tempo by a jot. The love of order was the very core of him. His apartment almost seemed to clean itself, the quiet and orderly way in which he went about the work of keeping it so, gave no sense of effort, no sense of care or worry. It was as if everything he did was as natural to him as his breath, and was a kind of pleasure.

First, he went into his gleaming white-tiled bathroom, opened the cabinet, took out his tooth brush and tooth powder, brushed his teeth, put everything back just as he had found it, and washed out the bowl. Then he took a shower—first a warm one, then a tepid one, and then a cold one—but not too cold. He had serious misgivings concerning the sudden shock of icy water upon the frail small beating of the—heart. Then he dried himself vigorously with a bath-towel, put on his dressing-gown and shaved himself, then cleaned and dried his razor carefully, washed out the brush, washed out the basin, and put everything back into the gleaming cabinet, spotless and shining, exactly as he had found them. Then he combed his hair; his hair was abundant, close cropped, dark blond in color, and George parted it into two neat, shining wings exactly in the center.

Then George came out of the bathroom, crossed the big room, opened up the chest of drawers, and took out fresh and neatly folded garments, socks, underwear, a shirt. He put them on, then opened the closet door, selected a suit of clothes from the row of well-cut, faultlessly-kept suits that hung there, and put it on. Then he selected a pair of shoes from the substantial assortment in the closet, selected with great care a tie marked with a fine gray stripe, adjusted arm-bands of ruffled blue to keep his sleeves up, and now was ready for his breakfast.

George entered his gleaming kitchenette, and with unhurried method, set about the preparation of his morning meal. First, he filled a glistening little pot with water, set it down upon the stove, and got the burner going. Then he filled the container of his drip-ma-chine with Sanka coffee, and screwed it into place. Then he opened the door of his gleaming electric ice box, took out two good-sized Florida oranges, cut them evenly in two, and squeezed their juice into a glass. The water on the stove was boiling now. George poured the water carefully into the round top of the drip-machine, and poured the remainder of the boiling water in the sink. Then while his Sanka coffee dripped, George put three slices of fresh bread into the electric toaster on the breakfast table, set out a knife and fork, a cup and saucer, a square of butter and a napkin, set his glass of orange juice beside the plate, and in faultless taste, impeccable spotlessness, pre-pared to have a breakfast—with himself.

George drank the orange juice, consumed the buttered toast, and slowly swallowed down a cup of Sanka coffee.

Then he cleared the table, washed the dishes and put each article back into its gleaming cabinet, washed out the sink, wiped off the table, then went out into his bed-and-living room. George opened the door of a closet in his little entrance hall, took out a mop, an oil mop, a broom, a dustpan and a dusting cloth, and brought them back with him. First he swept the floor of his little kitchenette and dining alcove. Then he swept the three small rugs, and went over the wax-polished floor carefully with the oil mop. Then he took the water-mop, and carefully swabbed the glittering tiling of the bath-room floor. Then he took the soft dust cloth, and very tenderly and lovingly, went over every square inch of the magnificent grand piano. Then he took all the sheets and covers from his couch, put the sheets on tidily, spread the thin gray blanket over them and tucked it in, covered the whole couch with the blue coverlet, took certain plump and tidy-looking cushions from the closet, and arranged them taste-fully. Then he stood for a moment in the center of his spotless little universe, with a quiet look of satisfaction upon his face, like the Lord of some small but immaculate creation, who looks upon his work and finds it good.

In the midst of these pleasing contemplations, the telephone rang. George jumped as if he had been shot.

The sharp electric *thring* of the telephone bell had cut across the calm weather of his spirit like a lightning flash. The telephone rang again—again—again—insistent and emphatic, naked as a live wire. George felt his knees give under him, he cast distracted looks about the room, he looked at the telephone as if it were a venomous reptile. Good God, was there no escape, no means by which a man could make himself secure against all the brutal shocks of this huge world? He had burnt all bridges, closed all avenues, built his walls more cunningly than those of Troy, and still the remorseless and inevitable tides of life came in.

But why—for what reason—should his 'phone ring now? No one ever called him in the morning. Swiftly his mind ran over the list of all the people that he knew who were privileged to call. There were only eleven people in the world to whom, after years of cautious acquaintanceship, he had revealed his number.

Even with these people he had never felt entirely free. Moreover, he had never allowed the whole chosen eleven to know one another: he kept them carefully parcelled in three groups. One group—a group of four—were people who shared his interest in music; he went to concerts with them, to the symphony, occasionally to opera. A second group, a group of three, were Bridge players, and George was an excellent hand at Bridge. The third group, also of four people, were Theatre Goers. George enjoyed the theatre, and for eight months of the year went once a week. Thus even in his well-ordered social life, George still displayed his salutary caution: none of the Concert Attenders knew any of the Bridge players, and none of the Bridge players had ever met any of the Theatre Goers, just as none of the Theatre Goers had ever heard of the existence of the Concert Attenders.

But these eleven people were the only ones to whom he had confided the number of his telephone. And none of them, he knew, would dream of calling him at this hour of the morning, unless something of a catastrophic nature had occurred.

Then—George stared desperately at that crackling instrument of dread—who could it be, then?—*Who*?

He was more composed now, steeled with resolution, and when at last he took the instrument from the hook, his voice was cadenced to its customary tone of quiet, deep, and pleasant courtesy.

"Hello—Hello!"

"Oh, hello darling. Is it *really* you? I was about to give up hope."

Her voice was husky, full of depth, the cadences of unuttered tenderness, conveying perfectly a sense of quiet irony, and affection —the full image of its owner's loveliness. But George, just at the moment, was in no fit mood to estimate its beauty; the voice had gone through him in a searing flash of memory—he was white around the lips, and leaning forward, gripping the instrument with a hand gone bloodless to the fingertips, he stammered hoarsely:

"Hello, hello—Who is it?—Is it—"

"Guess who, darling?" The quiet irony in the husky tone had deepened just a trifle.

"Margaret!" he gasped. "Is that *you*!"

"That's who. You seem a little overcome, my dear," the husky tone was dulcet now.

"Why—why—yes—no—that is," George stammered with an uncertain laugh—"*Yes!* I was a little surprised. I wonder how . . ." he stopped abruptly, fumbled, trying to get out of it.

"How *what*? How I got your number?"

"Why—why—yes! That is—I gave instructions to the company not to let anyone—" he reddened with embarrassment, then blurted out "—of course, I wanted *you* to have it—I—I—I've been intending all along to write and tell you the new number—"

"You *have*?" the husky voice was faintly accented with cynical amusement. "Only it's just escaped your mind during the past two or three years, hasn't it?"—

"Well—you see—" he fumbled.

"I know, darling. It's all right. You're a very secret little boy now-a-days, aren't you?" another pause, a brief one, but for George a very long one. "Well, since you're so curious to know, I'll tell you how I got the number. Stew Taylor gave it to me."

"But he—" George began, puzzled.

"Yes, I know he didn't," the low voice was shaded now with sadness. "You've covered your tracks pretty well these last three years. Stew happened to meet one of your Bridge-playing friends, and he let him have it."

"But he *couldn't*!" George said incredulously. "I—I mean he *wouldn't*—that is—"

"Well, he did, my love. It's too bad, but there's no telling what a few drinks will do, is there?"

"Well, whoever it was," George began angrily, "I'd like to find out —because when I gave those numbers out, I told people not to— well, anyway," he broke off, "it's nice to hear from you again, Margaret. We've got to try—"

"Try what? To get together sometime. Yes, I know," the irony of the voice was very quiet now—"I've been trying for the last three years."

"Well, then," he said quickly, "that's what we'll have to do—I'll call you up sometime when—"

"When I'm not looking? Or when I'm dead?"

"Now, Margaret," said George, laughing and speaking in his familiar quiet voice, "you know you're not being fair when you say that. I've been meaning to call you for a long time. Just at present—" he coughed a little, and looked quickly at his watch—"well, anyway, when things slacken up a little—"

"When things slacken up a little? You sound frightfully busy. What's the matter?—have you taken up crocheting?"

"Well, you see—"

"I don't want to take up your valuable time, you know. Have you finished with your daily housekeeping yet?"

"Well—*yes*!" he confessed.

"Had your breakfast?"

"Yes. Oh, yes."

"Washed the dishes?"

"Yes."

"Tidied up the kitchen, and put everything away in his little cubby-hole?"—the husky voice suspiciously dulcet now.

"Yes—but look here—"

"Tidied up the bathroom, swept the floors, dusted the furniture—"

"Look here, Margaret. What are you trying to—"

"Made up his little bed, and spread the cute little cover on it, and plumped the cosy little pillows out—"

"Well, what's the matter with all that?" he protested.

"*Matter*?"—innocently—"Why, darling, I didn't say anything was the matter. I think it's *wonderful*!"

"Well, I don't see it's anything for you to make fun of," he said sulkily.

"Make *fun* of—"innocently aggrieved.—"But who's making *fun*? I think you're *won*-derful! You can do *everything*! You can keep house, make up beds, wash dishes, sweep floors, keep everything tidy as a pin," piously the voice enumerated these virtues.

"Well, if you're going to be funny about—"

"And play the piano, and play Bridge—" the voice continued dulcetly—"Oh, *yes*!"—eagerly, excitedly—"And he can *cook*, too! He's a *good* cook, isn't he?" After a moment, slowly, laughingly, the husky tone now carrying its full charge of sarcasm, she concluded: "My, my! I wonder if they know what they're missing?"

"What *who's* missing?" said George suspiciously.

"What the *girls* are missing—" then, sweetly, tenderly, the coup-de-grace: "You'd make a great little mother to some woman's children, Georgy. Don't you know you would?"

"It seems to me—" said George—"Look," he continued quietly, "I'm going to hang up."

"Oh, wait," she said; the woman's husky voice was suddenly subdued to earnest tenderness—"Don't go away. I mean, what I wanted to say was, why couldn't we"—the voice had changed to jesting irony again—"Get on your running shoes, darling—what are you going to be doing tonight?"

He was silent, stunned; and then he floundered:

"Why—why—I—I've—I'm going to the theatre with some people that I know."

"I see . . . And tomorrow night, darling?"—the voice was dulcet now: knowing the tone, he reddened, squirmed, remembered the look in her eye.

"Why—tomorrow," George said slowly, "I—I've promised some friends to play Bridge."

"Ah-hah"—just barely audible—"And the day *after* tomorrow, my sweet?"

"Why—now let's see," George mumbled, fumbling desperately for time—"I've promised some people I know to go to a piano recital."

"And Friday?"

"Why—Friday," George began desperately—"I—I've—"

"I know," the husky voice broke in sweetly—"Friday is fish day, isn't it, and you've promised some Catholic friends of yours to go to a clambake, haven't you?—"

"Now, Margaret," George began, with a troubled laugh—"You know—"

"Of course I know, my pet—on Saturday you're going out to the country for the weekend, to visit some 'people you know'—aren't you? And by the way, who are all these 'people you know' anyway? Most of the people you used to know never see you any more."

"Well—you see—"

"Look here," she said quietly—"What's happened to you, anyway? What's wrong with you?—What are you afraid of, anyway? . . . There wasn't one of us five years ago who wouldn't have bet his last nickel upon you—upon everything we thought you were going to do in the world—"

"Oh, wait a minute—" he put in quietly—"I wasn't a genius—and I never pretended to be one."

"No, I know you weren't—But you did have something that is not given to one person in a thousand—the power to feel and know music and to play it in such a way that you could give to other people some of your own feeling. That was a gift that came straight to you from God—and what have you done with it?"

"Now, Margaret," his own voice was hot and angry now—"if that's what you're going to—"

"I'll tell you what you've done with it!"—Her voice cut harshly in across the wire—"You've thrown it away because you got scared, because you were afraid to use it, and what have you got left? Well, you've got your Bridge-playing friends, and your little apartment, and your little music students, haven't you?"

"If you're going to sneer at the way I earn my living—"

"Oh, I couldn't sneer at it sufficiently," she said. "I couldn't begin to sneer at it the way it deserves to be sneered at!"

"If you mean to say," he began in a choking voice, "that you think the way I earn my living is not honorable—"

"Oh, honorable, my eye!" she said wearily. "So is ditch-digging! Look here, George Hauser—there are a thousand things that you could do that would be honorable—making kiddy cars or peddling toy balloons. But what you ought to do is the work that you were put here for!"

"Apparently you think, then," he began stiffly, "that teaching young men and women that show signs of musical talent—"

"Oh, talent, my eye!" she said coarsely again. "You know perfectly well that it doesn't matter in the slightest what happens to most of them—whether they learn to play the mouth-harp or the accordion—"

"There," he said frigidly, "I cannot agree with you. I assure you that I have some young people of talent who—"

"Well, what if you have?" she said brutally. "Let them get along with their talent as best they may!—Let someone else show them what to do! It's about time you started worrying about *your* talent! Oh George, George, what in the name of God has happened to you? You used to be so different! Don't you know that everyone adored you—they do still? Have you forgotten the good times we used to have together?—Stew Taylor, Kate, myself, the Crosbys, Buzz Wilton, Doris, you?—What's come over you?—Have you forgotten the time you said, 'Let's go to Brooklyn'—and we went, not knowing where—the times we used to ride back and forth across the Staten Island Ferry—the time you asked the policeman where Red Hook was—and he tried to keep us from going—the times we went to Shorty Gallini's on Sixth Avenue—all of the times we stayed up talking all night long—what's happened to you, George? Have you forgotten all of them?"—

"You know," he said slowly—"there was something—I found out—"

There was a pause.

"Oh, yes, I know," she said quietly, with the shadow of a weary irony, "there was your—heart. You were always bothered by it, weren't you? The college doctor in Ann Arbor told you to take care of it, didn't he?"

"Margaret," George said gravely, "if you knew what you—"

"Oh, darling, but I know. The doctor told you that you ought to watch your heart—and so you watched it. You told me all about your heart—do you remember?—How frail the heart was—how easy it was for the heart to stop beating."

"Those," said George, "are very serious—"

"Do you know something, George—" she now said slowly.

"What?"

"Well, I'll tell you"—very slowly—"Some day you're going to *die* of—*heart*-failure—"

"Oh, *Margaret!*" he gasped.

"You're *going* to die of heart-*failure*," she repeated slowly—"Some day your heart is going to *fail*—it's just going to quit—lie down—stop—"

"*Margaret!*"

"—Like *mine*, and like Stew Taylor's, Kate's, Buzz Wilton's—all the rest of us—"

"Yes, but—"

"Listen: what's it all about?—this business of your heart? We know about your heart, and really George, your heart was not so bad. I used to listen to it in the nighttime when I slept with you—"

"*Margaret!*"

"Oh, but I did—and really, George, your heart was just a—*heart*."

"Margaret, if you're going to—"

"Oh, but I did—I happen to remember—and really, George, your heart was not so bad, until little what's-her-name—the little washed-out blonde with the hank of hair—came along, and took you for a ride."

"Now, Margaret, you look here—"

"—The little ex-chorine who got money from you for her boy friend—ran away with him and came back broke—broke down, confessed, worked on your sympathies—"

"Now, you look here—"

"—And got more money from you for her boy friend.—"

"I'm not going to—"

"—Oh, you're not going to what? You had fine friends, a fine career, and everyone adored you and believed in you—you had me, and I'm a nice woman—and you gave everything, all of us, the gate for a little washed-out ex-chorine who gave *you* the gate—"

"Listen, if you think—"

"—And walked all over that poor *heart* of yours, didn't she?"

"You can—"

"I can what? I can go to hell, you mean? Well, why not? You've sold us out—your friends, yourself, your work—but you've discovered that you have a—heart. So we can go to hell, can't we?"

When George spoke, his voice was quiet, deep, sincere, and sad. "If you feel that way," he said, "I don't see why you bother to call me up."

There was a moment's pause, then the husky voice suddenly charged through with passion:

"Because, you God-damned fool, I happen to adore you!"

The receiver banged up in his face.

When George got up, his face was white and his hands were shaking. He walked over to the mantel of his room, without knowing where he was going or what he was doing. He leaned upon the mantel. Above him was the picture of a river. It was George's river; the upper reaches of the Mississippi in the State of Minnesota. It was a silvery stream that channeled around islands—there were dense woodings of great trees upon the shore, there were long wooded buttes, high promontories, also with the lovely forestings of the great trees dense. In his quiet face, he knew there was the look that one often finds among people who come from this part of the country. It was neither sad nor resigned, but unconsciously it had sadness, resignation in it: what it *really* had, he knew, was a gigantic acceptance, a sense of quiet and enormous *background*, a sense of great scenes gone home to the heart, the hush of the enormous evenings and the gigantic distances, of something immense, and waiting, set there in the silence of repose. He knew this was the way he looked. And his river also looked like this. He had swum in it when young, looked at it a thousand times, known every part of the immense landscapes of its shores. It was his, his country, his America—and his river. But now he was finished with that, too.

That, he knew, had been *his* river. And for him, at least, it had been a good deal more than river, a good deal more than an aspect of familiar geography. It was, in a way, the image of his whole life; his life had been haunted by that river; it had wound through the landscape of his youth like a haunted thread. In so many ways past knowing and past telling, he knew that this great stream—was his. It was so calm, so homely, so mysterious—like so much else that we have known here, itself a part of the "large unconscious scenery" of this country, so familiar and so strange, so friendly and so indefinably sad—as if, in the utter plainness of our best-known things, there is something undefined and troubling, that plain speech can never know—something at which men can only guess, which comes to pass across a quiet spirit like a troubling light, and to vanish before it can be outlined or defined—Oh, hard and strange enigma of the lonely land! *This* had been his. He, too, had known it, but now—no more!

In a few minutes, when he had grown quieter, he went over and sat down at his piano and began to play grave and tranquil music; he played the Chopin C Minor Prelude; he smote the keys with strong white fingers, and the music came.

The bell rang. George stopped midway among the calm resounding chords. He went to the door and opened it. Ledig, the Superintendent of the building, was standing there.

"Good morning, Ledig," George greeted the man in his deep and pleasant tone. "Come in."

Ledig was a man of George's age—in the late thirties—with the common, square, and friendly-brutal face of the Germanic stock, and eyes of china-blue.

"Good morning, Mr. Hauser," Ledig said, and grinned, "I just t'ought I'd speak to you about de apartment—"

"Oh, yes," said George quietly, and waited.

Ledig looked around the room, his round eyes surveyed the scene approvingly; George was his favorite tenant.

"You got it goot here," Ledig said. "You keep it nice."

A quick communication passed between them—one of pleasure and swift understanding; George said nothing.

"—about de apartment—you haf deceit-ed?" Ledig asked.

"Yes, Ledig," George answered in his deep and tranquil tone, "I have decided."

"And," said Ledig earnestly, "you vant de udder vun?"

"Yes, Ledig," George said, as before, "I want the other one."

"It is on de udder seit, dough, Mr. Hauser," Ledig said, then added doubtfully, "But you like besser, de udder seit?"

"Yes, Ledig, I think I'll like it better on the other side," said George.

"But," said Ledig very earnestly, "de udder seit, Mr. Hauser, it gifs no more riffers."

"No, that is true," said George in his low and quiet tone.

"But," Ledig's blue eyes were full of puzzled trouble, "you like it besser dat vay, den—mit no more riffers?"

"Yes," said George, "I like it better that way, Ledig."

"But," the china eyes were fuller still of puzzled wonder and regret.

"No more *riffers*, Mr. Hauser."

When Ledig had gone, George stood there leaning on the mantel. For a moment he regarded the picture of his river with quiet eyes. Then he walked to the window and looked out. Upon that shining tide of life, a boat was passing. George lowered the Venetian blinds. And suddenly the room was dark with morning.

Now there were no more rivers.

Index